Aeneas J. G. Mackay

Memoir of John Major of Haddington

A study in Scottish history and education

Aeneas J. G. Mackay

Memoir of John Major of Haddington
A study in Scottish history and education

ISBN/EAN: 9783337240790

Printed in Europe, USA, Canada, Australia, Japan

Cover: Foto ©ninafisch / pixelio.de

More available books at **www.hansebooks.com**

JOHN MAJOR OF HADDINGTON

'At nescio qua natale solum dulcedine cunctos ducit et immemores non sinit esse sui.'

> Dedication by JOHN MAJOR of the Edition of his Commentary, '*In Quartum Librum Sententiarum Petri Lombardi*,' to ALEXANDER STEWART, Archbishop of St. Andrews, 1509.

(*Fifty Copies Printed*)

MEMOIR OF
JOHN MAJOR
OF HADDINGTON

DOCTOR OF THEOLOGY IN THE UNIVERSITY
OF PARIS: AFTERWARDS REGENT IN THE
UNIVERSITIES OF GLASGOW AND SAINT
ANDREWS AND PROVOST OF THE
COLLEGE OF ST. SALVATOR

1469-70—1550

A Study in

Scottish History and Education, By

Æ. J. G. MACKAY

LL.D., ADVOCATE

EDINBURGH

Privately Printed by T. and A. Constable
at the University Press
1892

NOTE

THE references to the Appendix will be found in the Translation of John Major's *History of Greater Britain*, by Archibald Constable (Scottish History Society), as an Introduction to which, this *Memoir*, originally delivered as an Address to the Students of the University of St. Andrews, has been printed.

LIFE OF JOHN MAJOR

JOHN MAJOR or MAIR was born in 1469-70, the eleventh year of the reign of James III., at Gleghornie, now a farmhouse, perhaps then a hamlet, in the parish of North Berwick, about two miles inland from Tantallon[1], the castle of the Douglases, and three miles from Hailes[2], the castle of the Hepburns, to both of which families, though himself of humble origin, his talents introduced him. Crawford, the historiographer, in the Life prefixed to Freebairn's edition of Major's History, dates his birth as early as 1446, and Dr. Mackenzie, in his *Lives of Scots Writers*, as late as 1478; but he corrects this in the preface to his second volume from information he had received from Paris, and assigns 1469 as the true date. A passage in one of Major's works proves that he was really born in 1469-70, for he states in the preface to a new edition, published in 1519, that he had then reached the confines of his forty-ninth year; and this is confirmed by the fact that he graduated as Doctor in Theology at Paris in 1505, a degree which could not be taken under the age of thirty-five[3]. Major was alive in 1549, when he was excused from attending

Major's birth, 1469-70.

---

[1] Appendix II., p. 437.   [2] Appendix II., p. 425.
[3] I am indebted to Mr. Archibald Constable for directing my attention to this passage: 'Licet enim Martinus Magister [*i.e.* Martin le Maistre] quæstione penultima de temperantia dicat seniores junioribus in re scholastica invidere; non sum de numero juniorum; *nam hoc libro absoluto quadragesimi noni anni fimbrias aggredior.*'—Johannis Majoris in exordio prælectionis lib. quarti sententiarum ad auditores propositio. See Appendix II., p. 437. This Preface is not printed in the earlier editions of 1509 and 1516. Mr. Hume Brown has supplied me with the further corroboration of this date that a degree in theology could not be then taken at Paris before the age of 35. It is due, however, to Dr. Mackenzie, a writer somewhat unfairly disparaged, to mention that he arrived at the true date of Major's birth in the correction made in the Preface to the second volume of his *Lives of Scots Writers*.

a Provincial Council at Edinburgh on account of his age, and died in that or the following year, when his successor as Provost of the College of St. Salvator at St. Andrews was appointed. His long life of seventy-nine years was thus passed in the century which preceded the Scottish Reformation, a memorable period in the history of Scotland and of Europe.

At Gleghornie, near North Berwick. He refers to Gleghornie as his birthplace in the History[1], and styles himself 'Glegornensis' in the titles of several of his other works. In his quaint manner, when he mentions any event which occurred near North Berwick, he notes the precise distance, a token that he retained an affectionate recollection of his early home. The oatcakes baked on the girdle over the ashes, the mode of grinding meal and brewing beer, the way of catching crabs and lobsters at North Berwick, the habits of the Solan Geese of the Bass, the popular superstitions still current in the most civilised part of Scotland[2], even the exact time at North Berwick, are described with the close observation of a frequent eye-witness, and leave little doubt that he was born in one of the thatched cottages whose fragile character he deplores[3], and was the son of one of the labourers, or perhaps one of the small farmers, probably of some church lands in the neighbourhood. It is possible his father was the tacksman of Gleghornie itself, whom he uses as an illustration in a passage of his Commentary on the Fourth Book of the Sentences of Peter Lombard[4]. But of his parents or descent nothing is certainly known. A boy of parts in that age, however humble his parentage, had opportunities of distinguishing himself if he chose Learning or the Church as his profession. A

---

[1] *History*, I. vi. pp. 33-4.

[2] Dubitatur adhuc : Isti Fauni et vocati *brobne* [*brownies*] apud nos domi qui non nocent, ad quod propositum talia faciunt. Respondetur : multa referuntur de talibus : ut proterere tantum tritici in una nocte vel sicut xx. viri terere possunt. Projiciunt lapillos inter sedentes prope ignem ruri, ridere videntur, et similia facere. Insuper dubitatur : an possunt futura predicere ; et movetur dubitatio. Sunt aliqui apud nostrates Britannos qui more prophetico futura predicunt utpote de morte et homicidio aliquorum.—*Expos. in Matt.*, ed. 1518, fol. xlviii.

[3] *History*, I. v. p. 30. [4] Dist. xv. Quæst. 45.

pious reference to the custom of his childhood amongst the
country-folk of Scotland, that when the children went to bed
they asked their parents' blessing with outstretched hands, and
the father gave it with God's blessing added, shows one part of
his education had begun at home [1].

His name is a common one in Scotland; indeed in the Latin His name.
form of Major it is known in England and on the Continent.
It may have been derived from the office of Maor (*Scotice*
Mair) or serjeant, the executive official of the Celtic thane, who
remained attached to the court of the sheriff; or, more probably,
in Lothian it meant no more than 'elder', when, surnames
coming into use, it was necessary to distinguish between two
persons of the same Christian name. It is noticeable that in
several of the entries in the Registers of Paris, Glasgow, and
St. Andrews, he is described as 'Johannes (*i.e.* filius) Major*is*'[2],
as if his father had first assumed the surname. Whether he
owed it to his parents, or to the monks who detected his aptness
for learning, Major received the rudiments of a good education
in his own neighbourhood, almost certainly at the school of
Haddington, already noted amongst the schools of Scotland, At school at Haddington.
where a little later John Knox was a scholar. In remem-
brance of this, in some of his works he describes himself as
'Hadingtonanus', and in the dedication of his treatise on the
Fourth Book of the Sentences to Gavin Douglas, Bishop of Dunkeld, and Robert Cockburn, Bishop of Ross, he makes the following grateful reference to his connection with Haddington and its
school:—'These reasons have led me to dedicate this work to
you, for not only is each of you like myself a Scottish Briton
[*Scotus Britannus*], but also my nearest neighbour in my native
land. The Dialogue in the Preface to my treatise on the First
Book explains the distance from the birthplace of one of you

---

[1] *Ibid.* Dist. xxiii. Quæst. 2.

[2] So Prantl in his *Geschichte der Logik*, iv. 217, throughout calls Major Johannes Majoris. But I incline to think, on a view of the whole evidence, that this is merely from his name usually appearing on the title-pages of his works in the genitive case.

[Gavin Douglas, who was born at Tantallon] is not more than a Sabbath-day's journey. Haddington has a still fuller right to rejoice in the origin of the other [Robert Cockburn], the town which fostered the beginnings of my own studies, and in whose kindly embraces I was nourished as a novice with the sweetest milk of the art of grammar, and carried on in my education to a pretty advanced age [*longiuscula ætas*], and it is not more than five miles from Gleghornie where I was born. So that many persons call me not wrongly a Haddington man. Besides, I have enjoyed the friendly and familiar society of you both, at home as well as at Paris, and have been honoured by your public commendation, of which I cannot speak fully in few words. Therefore, as Sallust says of Carthage, "I prefer to be silent rather than say too little". For these causes I have determined to dedicate this work to you, which I pray you to review not with severe and harsh eyebrows, but with the benignant and modest countenances habitual to you. Farewell. Paris, in the College of Montague, the Kalends of December 1516.'

That he was one of the youths of humble origin his country has often produced, eager to learn, patient in study, fond of argument, and of comparison, with what is called an inquisitive intellect, is proved by his subsequent career.

Before 1493 in north of England or the Borders.

A curious but tantalising reference in his History as to his personal experience informs us that Major spent seven years in the north, or more probably the borders[1], of England. When defending his country from the charge of poverty, on the ground that oatmeal was a common diet (for long before Dr. Johnson this was a vulgar scoff), he remarks: 'It is the food of almost all the natives of Wales and of the northern English, as I know from my own seven years' experience of that people [*ut a septennio expertus sum*[2]], as well as of the Scottish peasantry, and yet the main strength of the Scottish

---

[1] A somewhat minute knowledge of the Borders between England and Scotland is shown in his *History*, I. v. p. 19.

[2] Perhaps the meaning is 'as I have known by experience for seven years',

and English armies is in the peasantry—a proof that oat bread is not a thing to be laughed at.'

But as he positively states in the Dedication of his edition of Aristotle's Ethics to Wolsey [1] that he first crossed the Borders when he went through England to Paris in 1493, it would seem that he considered Gleghornie on the Borders,—a flexible term at this period of internecine raids, and his acquaintance with the habits of the English may have been derived from the Northumberland moss-troopers.

He chose the vocation of a travelling scholar, an excellent combination of the Middle Ages, in many respects preferable to the more sedentary training of modern times. His name does not appear as a student at either of the Scottish universities then founded, in both of which he was afterwards a teacher, but before 1493, when already a man of twenty-three, he found his way to Cambridge. That university, though somewhat inferior to Oxford in numbers and reputation, as he notes with a candour creditable to a Cambridge man, and in spite of the attractions of Baliol College, possibly because of the dislike of North-countrymen which was a tradition of mediæval Oxford, was then a favourite school for Scottish students. George Wishart, the first of the Scottish Reformers, was not long after a student at Corpus Christi, in the same university.

He studied for a year, but attended lectures apparently only for three months [2], at God's House, the earlier foundation converted into Christ's College in 1505. He selected it for a reason strange to us, but at that time natural, because it was situated in the parish of St. Andrew [3], the patron saint of Scotland, and of the diocese to which Major himself belonged. The church dedicated to that saint still stands opposite the College gate over which, as at St. John's, the other foundation of the Lady Margaret, the mother of Henry VII. and grand-

1493, at God's House, Cambridge.

---

but this scarcely removes the puzzle of the passage, as Major had been in England long before 1518, the date when his History was written.

[1] See Appendix II., p. 448.   [2] *History*, I. v. p. 25.   [3] *Ibid.*

mother of Margaret, wife of James IV., the Tudor arms are boldly sculptured. It may have been a consequence of this portion of his education that he became through life a strenuous advocate of the union of Scotland with England. The higher culture and refinement of English life certainly made an impression on the country-bred Scot.

'While I was a student at Cambridge,' he says in one of the sidenotes which relieve the dry style of his History, 'during the great festivals I spent half the night awake listening to the bells. The university is on a river, so from the undulation of the water their sound is sweeter.' With the freedom from prejudice which was one of his characteristics, he remarks that the bells of St. Oseney, the cradle of Oxford, 'are the best in England, and that as in music the English excel all nations, so they excel in the sweet and artistic modulation of their bells'[1].

'No village of forty houses is without fine bells. In every town of any size you hear the sweetest chimes from terce to terce.' He enlarges, and, as his manner is, generalizes from his observations, the minuteness of which is noteworthy: 'although you may find a few as finished musicians in Scotland as in England, there are not nearly so many of them[2].'

These remarks, intended for the ear of his own countrymen, to prompt them to the study and practice of music, have been long in bearing fruit. To a Scottish student returning from the English universities, the bells of his native town are not yet such as he would willingly lie awake to hear, and still too often recal by contrast the chimes of the churches and college

---

[1] *History*, III. i. p. 110.
[2] *Ibid.* I. iv. p. 27, with which compare I. v. p. 30, where he laments that the Scottish priests were ignorant of the Gregorian Chant, and his statement (VI. xiv. p. 366) that James I. learned music in England. 'Bells were not universal in parish churches in Scotland even at the end of last century. It often happened that there was nowhere to hang them: a theologian of 1679 inveighs against "that pitiful spectacle, bells hanging upon trees for want of bell houses."'—Joseph Robertson, *Scottish Abbeys and Cathedrals*, p. 102.

LIFE OF JOHN MAJOR

chapels on the banks of the Isis or the Cam, the sweet changes rung in the towers of St. Mary in both universities, or of Christ Church, where the bells of Oseney Priory are said to have found a home in the Gatehouse tower.

From Cambridge Major passed in 1493 to Paris, probably his original destination. Paris was then, especially for theologians, the most famous university in Europe. Its colleges were crowded with students from almost all countries, even the distant extremities of Europe—Scandinavia, Spain, Scotland—as yet without complete universities of their own. There were as many as 10,000 at the lowest estimate. But national jealousy and the growth of Oxford and Cambridge had recently withdrawn the English students, and the Scotch who continued to frequent it were now enrolled in the *Natio Alemanica* (or German) which had been substituted for the older name of the *Natio Anglicana*. Before he crossed the Channel Major had probably visited Oxford as well as Cambridge, and his brief notes on the universities[1] and a few of the principal towns in England, which bear marks of personal observation, deserve notice, as there are few diaries of intelligent travellers in the end of the fifteenth century now extant[2]. 'Londinum', he says, 'which was called by the Britons London, is situated on the Thames, a river thrice the size of the Seine at Paris. It is visited by the ships of all nations, and has a very fine bridge and church. One mile to the west lies Westminster, where there is a royal palace, the monuments of the kings, and the seat of justice. Three miles to the East is Greenwich the royal port, where you may see in abundance barges passing up to London and down to the sea with sails or the tide. London elects a wealthy and senior tradesman yearly as Mayor, before whom a

Description of the English Towns and Universities.

---

[1] He more than once refers to Oseney Priory. The long list of the famous men who had studied at Oxford and the comparison between the colleges at the two Universities indicate a knowledge of both.

[2] *History*, I. v. p. 21.

sword is carried as an emblem of justice, whose duty it is if corn is dear to import it to lower the price. It exceeds Rouen, the second city of France, in population, but is far before it in wealth. It is enriched by being the seat of justice, the almost constant residence of the king, and by the affluence of its merchants. Some Englishmen, with whom I agree, count the population of Paris three times that of London, but it is not three times as wealthy. In the Thames there are three or four thousand tame swans; but', he adds with characteristic caution, 'I merely repeat what was told me, for, though I have seen, I have never counted them. York is the second city of England, the see of an archbishop, distant fifty leagues from Scotland, a town of large extent, but not rich or populous, through the want of the three advantages London has. The third city is Norwich, an Episcopal See, in which that kind of cloth called Ostade is manufactured, both single and double. There are other considerable cities,—as Bristol; Coventry, a good town without a river, which is remarkable; Lincoln, formerly famous, and many more[1]. England has two famous universities: Oxford, celebrated abroad, which has produced eminent philosophers and theologians, as Alexander Hales, Richard Middleton, John Duns the Doctor Subtilis, Ockham, Adam the Irishman, Strode, Bradwardine, and others[2].' Of its colleges he names Magdalen and New as the foremost, each with a hundred bursaries—some in divinity and others in arts. 'The other university is Cambridge, a little inferior to Oxford in number of students and reputation for letters.' Of its colleges he mentions King's, which may be compared with New College, Oxford; Queens'; a Royal Hall—inferior to Queens'

---

[1] The somewhat eccentric list of English towns mentioned by Major is probably accounted for by the fact that in each of them there was a Franciscan monastery.

[2] See note *Hist.* I. v. p. 23, as to the philosophers named by Major, fourteen in all, of whom it is noticeable that at least eight were Franciscans.

College—the future Trinity, not yet risen to the dignity of a College; Christ's College, where he studied himself, and Jesus, formerly a convent for women, reformed by Doctor Stubbs[1], the nuns having been ejected. 'I approve', he adds, 'of this ejection, for if convents become houses of ill fame, good institutions must be put in their place.'

'The course of study in the English universities is seven or eight years before graduating as master in arts. They do not pay much attention to grammar. The government of the university is in the hands of a Chancellor, like the Rector of Paris elected yearly, and two Proctors who have jurisdiction over laymen as well as students. The number of students is 4000 or 5000, and though that of laymen [*i.e.* townsmen] is greater, they don't venture to rise against the students, who would soon put them down. The students are all adults, and carry swords and bows, being for the most part of good birth.'

He concludes this fragmentary but interesting sketch by praising the morality of the English in comparison with the Scottish ecclesiastics, and making one of the semi-ironical observations of which studious men are fond: 'For courage, prudence, and other virtues the English don't think they are the least nation in the world, and if they meet a foreigner who has parts or bravery, it is much to be regretted, they say, that he was not an Englishman.'

While the dates of Major's studies at Cambridge and visit to Oxford are not quite certain, the commencement of his curriculum at Paris is fixed by an entry in the Register of Matriculation in the University under the year 1493: 'Johannes Mair Glegornensis, Dioecesis S. Andreæ.' He commenced his course of Arts at the College of St. Barbe, of which Etienne

Paris, 1493. Studies Arts at College of St. Barbe.

---

[1] Stubbs is unknown to the historians of Cambridge, and the real reformer and founder of Jesus College was John Alcock, Bishop of Ely (Mullinger, p. 321), to whom Major refers in his Biblical Commentary.

Bonet[1], a philosopher and physician, was then principal, under John Boulac or Bouillache, curate of St. Jacques La Boucherie, afterwards Principal of the College of Navarre, and graduated as Licentiate in 1494 and as Master in 1496. His countryman, John Harvey[2], of the Scots College, was then Rector of the University, and Major held under him the honourable office of Procurator of the German Nation, and became its Quæstor or Treasurer in 1501. From the College of St. Barbe Major migrated at the suggestion of Natalis or Noel Beda[3], afterwards a celebrated leader of the Sorbonne, to the College of Montaigu, then under the government of a Fleming, John Standonk, who reformed it; and Standonk having been banished by Louis XII., Major, by the advice of Boulac, was affiliated to the College of Navarre[4], though he continued to teach philosophy as Regent in Arts in that of Montaigu at least down to and probably after the year 1505, when he graduated as Doctor of Theology. Remaining in Paris for twelve or thirteen years after his graduation he became one of its most famous Professors of Theology, as he had been formerly of Logic and Philosophy. It is probable, indeed, that he lectured simultaneously, as he certainly published his lectures in both Faculties during the same period (1509-1518).

The period of Major's residence in Paris was a marked epoch in the history of France and the University. It was the zenith of the Renaissance. The Revival of Learning, begun in Italy in the fourteenth and fifteenth centuries, had in the sixteenth crossed the Alps, and under the leadership of Erasmus taken root in France, England, Germany, and the Low Countries. It was the France of the last five years of Charles VIII. (1483-

Migrates to Montaigu.

Elected a Fellow of Navarre.

---

[1] As to the Principalship of Etienne Bonet, see Quicherat, *St. Barbe*, pp. 54-64. He was elected 1483, and died 1497.
[2] Of John Harvey I find no mention except in Mackenzie's *Lives of Scots Writers*, 2 Pref. p. 121.
[3] As to Noel Beda, see Hume Brown's *Memoir of Buchanan*, p. 69.
[4] Launoi: *Regiæ Navarræ Hist.* Op. iv. p. 396.

1498), of the reign of Louis XII. (1498-1515), and the first three years of Francis I. (1515-47), during which Major passed his life as Student, Regent in Arts, and Doctor in Theology in its capital. During these years the consolidation of the kingdom and the formation of modern France by the absorption of the great feudal houses was completed. Charles VIII. by marrying Anne, heiress of Brittany, united the French Wales to the Crown, and Louis XII. retained it, divorcing his wife Jane of France and marrying the widow of Charles. He added himself the large domains of the House of Orleans. Encouraged by the growth of their kingdom and the divisions of Italy, the French monarchs made the fatal attempt to annex parts of the peninsula where so many Frenchmen found their tombs. The survivors brought back the learning, arts, and manners of the more civilised but more luxurious south. History repeated with altered names the lines of Horace:— *[French history during Major's residence in France.]*

> ' Græcia capta ferum victorem cepit et artes
> Intulit agresti Latio.'

Italy, unlike Greece, was overrun, not subdued. In 1494 Charles VIII. marched through Rome to Naples; but his campaign was a triumph not a conquest. Louis XII. renewed the war, claiming Milan as well as Naples, for whose partition he entered into a league with Ferdinand of Aragon. That astute monarch succeeded in gaining the whole, and became in 1504 king of the Two Sicilies.

In 1508 along with Pope Julius II. the two ambitious kings joined in the League of Cambrai to crush the Republic of Venice, but the Pope suddenly deserted his French allies and made a new league, which he called the Holy League, to drive the French barbarians from Italy. Though Louis defeated the Spaniards at Ravenna the aid of the Swiss enabled the Pope to accomplish his purpose. The French quitted Italy before the death of Louis in 1515. His successor, Francis I., a young and hazardous monarch, engaged in a contest for the Imperial

Crown and the primacy of Europe with Charles v., who on the death of his grandfather Maximilian became emperor. Francis recovered Milan, but was taken prisoner at Pavia in 1525, and though he broke the treaty of Madrid and resumed the war in 1529 he was forced to relinquish Italy. While these events were occupying the politicians and armies of Europe, Scotland, which had been at peace with England during the reign of Henry VII., through the marriage of his daughter to James IV., quarrelled with Henry VIII., and lost her king by the fatal defeat of Flodden in 1513. Henry VIII. was too busy with his relations to the Continent to press his advantage. His aim as regards Scotland was to prevent the French alliance and maintain an ascendancy at the court of his sister's infant son. The failure of this aim was due largely to his sister, the mother of the king, and to Albany, a Frenchman in all but his name, who threw their influence into the scale in favour of France. The Regency of Albany led in 1523 to the renewal by the Scots of the Border War and the siege of Werk, the failure of which destroyed the prestige of the Regent.

Relations of England and Scotland.

During the period the history of which has been sketched in outline, France was both on political and educational grounds the natural resort of the Scottish student ambitious of carrying his studies to the highest point and sure of a hospitable reception from a nation which had never forgotten the ancient bonds that united Scotland and France. France as it then was is described in the beautiful verses of the great contemporary Scottish scholar, the pupil of Major, George Buchanan:

> 'At tu beata Gallia
> Salve! bonarum blanda nutrix artium,
> Orbem receptans hospitem atque orbi tuas
> Opes vicissim non avara impertiens,
> Sermone comis, patria gentium omnium
> Communis.'

Its Capital has been painted in a brilliant passage of a great French author of our day, who combined the knowledge of an antiquary and the imagination of a poet, with which we may enliven the prose of a biographic sketch.

In the fifteenth century, writes Victor Hugo[1], 'Paris was divided into three totally distinct and separate cities, each with its own physiognomy, individuality, manners, customs, privileges, and history: the *City*, the *University*, and the *Ville*. The *City*, which occupied the island, was the mother of the two others, like (forgive the comparison) a little old woman between two handsome strapping daughters. The *University* crowned the left bank of the Seine. . . . The *Ville*, the most extensive of the three divisions, stretched along the right bank. The *City*, properly so called, abounded in churches, the *Ville* contained the palaces, the *University* the colleges. The island was under the Bishop, the right bank under the Provost of Merchants, the left under the Rector of the University, the whole under the Provost of Paris, a royal not a municipal office.' Omitting details, let us fix our attention on the University, the part of Paris of which Major was a citizen, for foreign students acquired the rights, indeed more than the rights, of citizens, and the Scotch at this time those of nationality. *Paris in the 15th century.*

'The University brought the eye to a full stop. From the one end to the other it was a homogeneous compact whole. Three thousand roofs, whose angular outlines, adhering together, almost all composed of the same geometrical elements, seen from above, presented the appearance of a crystallisation. The forty-two colleges were distributed among them in a sufficiently equal manner. The curious and varied *The University*

---

[1] This bird's-eye view of Paris should be compared with the old plans and maps of the sixteenth century. Zeiller's views were taken in the middle of the seventeenth century, but two show Paris as it was in 1620, and are probably accurate representations of Paris as it was in Major's time. M. Adolphe Berty's 'Plan du Collège de St. Barbe et de ses environs vers 1480' is given in Quicherat's *St. Barbe*. The clever reconstruction by Mr. H. W. Brewer in Rose's *Life of Loyola* unfortunately places Montaigu College inaccurately. The description by Victor Hugo in the text has necessarily, but unfortunately, required to be condensed.

summits of these beautiful buildings were the productions of
the same art as the simple roofs they overtopped; in fact they
were but a multiplication by the square or cube of the same
geometrical figures. Some superb mansions made here and
there magnificent inroads among the picturesque garrets of the
left bank, the *Logis de Nevers* and *de Rouen,* which have been
swept away; the *Hôtel of Cluny,* which still exists for the
consolation of the artist. The Rouen palace had beautiful
circular arches. Near Cluny were the baths of Julian. There
were, too, many abbeys: the *Bernardines,* with their three
belfries; *St. Genevieve,* the square tower of which, still
extant, excites regret for the loss of the whole; the *Sorbonne,*
half college, half monastery, an admirable nave of which
still survives: the quadrangular cloister of the *Mathurins*;
its neighbour, the cloister of *St. Benedict*; the *Cordeliers,* with
their three enormous gables side by side; and the *Augustines'*
graceful steeple. The *Colleges,* an intermediate link between
the cloister and the world, formed the mean in the series of
buildings between the mansions and the abbeys, with an
austerity full of elegance, a sculpture less gaudy than that of
the palaces, less serious than that of the convents. Unfortunately scarcely any vestiges are left of edifices in which Gothic
art steered with such precision a middle course between
luxury and learning. The churches, both numerous and
splendid, of every age of architecture, from the circular arch
of *St. Julian* to the pointed ones of *St. Severin,* overtopped
all, and, like an additional harmony in this mass of harmonies,
shot up above the slashed gables, the open-work pinnacles and
belfries, the airy spires, whose line was a magnificent exaggeration of the acute angle of the roofs. The site of the University
was hilly. To the south-east the hill of *St. Genevieve* formed
an enormous wen, and it was a curious sight to see the
multitude of narrow winding streets now called *Le Pays Latin,*
those clusters of houses, which, scattered in all directions from

the summit of that eminence, confusedly covered its sides down to the water's edge, seeming, some of them to be falling down, others to be climbing up again, and all to be holding fast by one another.' The more minute geography of the *Pays Latin* has been learnedly described by M. Quicherat, from whom we learn that the College of Montaigu[1] stood at the angle between the Rue St. Etienne des Prés and the Rue des Sept Voies, having opposite to it on the other side of the latter street the small College de Portet, the Hotel de Marly, the Cemetery of the Poor Students, and the Great Gate of the Abbey of St. Genevieve[2]. At the back of the buildings of Montaigu ran a narrow lane appropriately called ' La Rue des Chiens', on the opposite side of which Montaigu possessed two small gardens bordering on the property of its rival, the College of St. Barbe, and the cause of frequent quarrels[3].

Site of Montaigu.

The Scottish student whose course we are attempting to follow, poring day and night over ponderous folios we now scarcely touch with the tips of our fingers, the commentators on Aristotle and the expounders of the Master of the Sentences, had little time to mark the minute features of the scene. Still, he breathed its air, and can scarcely have failed to receive some of the spirit which filled with pride most scholars, from whatever country they came. A few remembered with opposite feelings the hardships of the student. Erasmus was one of these. Buchanan too wrote a poem describing the miserable condition of the teachers of *Literae Humaniores* in Paris when without a post. But, returning seven years after from Portugal, his pen, which could flatter as well as satirise, celebrated the charms of Paris as those of a beloved mistress, and his return to happy France, the nurse of all good arts. One

---

[1] The site of Montaigu, of which some fragments still remained in 1861, is now occupied by the Bibliothèque de St. Geneviève.
[2] Quicherat's *Histoire de St. Barbe*, p. 17.
[3] *Ibid.* 25.

of its attractions with which Hugo closes his description cannot have escaped Major's musical ear:—' Behold at a signal proceeding from heaven, for the sun gives it, those thousand churches trembling all at once. You hear solitary tinkles pass from church to church; then see (for at times the ear too seems endowed with the power of sight) all of a sudden, at the same moment, how there rises from each steeple, as it were a column of sound, a cloud of harmony. At first the vibration of each bell rises straight, pure, separate; then, swelling by degrees, they blend, melt, and amalgamate into a magnificent concert. Say if you know anything in the world more rich, more dazzling, more gladdening, than this tumult of bells, this furnace of music, these ten thousand brazen tones breathed all at once from flutes of stone three hundred feet high, than that city which is but one orchestra, this symphony as loud as a tempest.'

Contrast of Paris and Edinburgh.

How different must this have been from the capital of Major's own country, the gray metropolis of the North, whose silence was broken not by harmony but by brawls, with one narrow street from the Castle to the Abbey, the backbone of a skeleton ribbed on either side with vennels, wynds, and closes, which ran on the north to the North Loch and its marshes, on the south to the lower level of the Cowgate, here and there varied by a small church, monastery, or hospital, but only with a collegiate church, St. Giles, for a Cathedral, the plain Tolbooth for a Palace of Justice, and Holyrood, recently built in imitation of a minor French Palace, for its Royal residence, as yet without a college, without mansions, and without walls, and numbering only some four or five thousand[1] houses, chiefly of wood. Yet, one who viewed the surrounding country from the low but noble hill, named after Arthur, guarding Edinburgh on the east, and let his eye follow the

---

[1] *History*, II. vi. p. 82. So the earlier editions of Froissart; but Buchon says the correct text is 400 or 500. The truth probably lies between these figures. But see footnote[1], p. 28.

curves of the Forth, with the Law of North Berwick and the Bass as its outlying forts, the sea-ports of Fife studding its northern margin; on the west the Castle Rock, rising sheer from the North Loch, the woods of the Dean or Den, Drumsheugh, and Corstorphine Hill; and on the south the slopes of the Braids succeeded by the Pentland Hills, with Highland mountain tops beyond the Forth closing the horizon, might claim for Edinburgh a natural site not inferior to Paris, fitting it to be the capital of the small country whose scenery it reproduced in miniature—the Loch, the River, and the Sea, the Moor, the Forest, and the Mountain. Greater than any external difference was the contrast between the intellectual barrenness of Edinburgh and Paris, the venerable museum of learning, the busy hive from which old and new ideas were swarming, to settle in all lands. The Scottish student in Paris passed from the schoolroom to the world, from solitary study to the society of colleges, whose number, Major notes, sharpens wits. The poorest became, as if by natural magic, a free citizen of the university, the mother of knowledge and eloquence, of the arts and sciences: the arts which so long had ruled the past; the sciences, yet unconscious of their young strength, which were to divide the empire of the future.

Montaigu College.

Three of these Colleges demand our special attention: Montaigu, where Major first taught in arts; Navarre, where, as well as at Montaigu, he lectured on the scholastic philosophy; and the Sorbonne, where he lectured on the scholastic divinity[1].

[1] 'The epithet of "last of the Schoolmen" is commonly given to Gabriel Biel, the summarizer of Ockham, who taught in Tübingen, and died in 1491. His title to it is not actually correct, and it might be more fitly borne by Francis Suarez, who died in 1617. But after the beginning of the fifteenth century scholasticism was divorced from the spirit of the times.'—Article SCHOLASTICISM, *Encyclop. Britannica*, 9th ed. The truth is, no one scholastic can be called the last. The method or form of philosophy so called died at different dates in different countries. A critic who has done me the favour to read this Introduction maintains it is not dead yet, but still taught in Romanist seminaries. It is sufficient for the present purpose to say that no English or Scottish Schoolman later than Major has a place in any of the leading histories of philosophy.

He was destined to be among the last of the schoolmen, the teachers of the old learning by the rigid scholastic discipline and methods. The new light of the revival of classical literature had already dawned. The Renaissance, or new birth, from which on the mother's side the Reformation or new form of creed and of morals was to spring, could not but affect the thoughts and opinions of those who were passing through manhood under its influence. To observe how this influence acted upon Major and his pupils gives the uneventful career of scholars a singular and unexpected interest.

The College of Montaigu, an old college of the beginning of the fourteenth century, founded by Ascelin, the Seigneur of that name, had fallen so low towards the end of the fifteenth, that it had only eleven shillings of rent for endowment, its buildings in ruins, and, as might be expected, scarcely any students. John Standonk, a native of Mechlin in Brabant, a man of humble origin, saw in its poverty an object for zeal, and an opportunity for a much-needed reform in the University. This remarkable man, whom Erasmus, no partial judge, describes as one 'whose temper you could not dislike, and whose qualifications you must covet, who, while he was very poor, was very charitable', after taking his degrees in arts and theology with distinction, though poverty forced him to read by moonlight in the belfry to save oil, was placed in this college by the Chapter of Notre Dame, its superior, in 1480, became its principal in 1483, and Rector of the University in 1485. He sought out the titles of its property which had been lost sight of, and secured new endowments, especially from Louis Malet, Sieur de Granville, Admiral of France. The constitution he introduced was based on rules of economy and asceticism resembling those of a monastery. He had seen with regret, continues Crévier, the historian of the University, whose narrative we abridge, ' that the bursaries founded for the poor had often been swallowed up by the rich, and determined to

Standonk's reforms.

found a College for the true poor, amongst whom, he remarked, were often to be found elevated spirits and happy natural parts, reduced by misery to a state unworthy of their genius, but who, if cultivated, might become great men and pillars of the Church. With this view, and to preserve the College from the invasion of the rich, he subjected his students to a hard life.' At first his scholars were sent to the Convent of the Chartreuse to receive, in common with beggars, the bread distributed at its gates. 'All the world knows', he proceeds, 'the frugal nourishment of these youths—bread, beans, eggs, herring, all in small quantity, and no meat. Besides, they had to keep all the Fasts,— that of Lent was kept also in Advent,—and on every Friday, as well as on special occasions. Nothing could be poorer than their dress and beds. They rose at cock-crow, constantly chanted the service of the Church, worked in the kitchen and refectory and cleaned the halls, the chapel, the dormitory, and the stairs. Their superior was called minister or servant of the poor, not by the too proud titles of master or principal. He received in this world only the cost of his living, dress, and of taking his degrees, exclusive of the *Doctorate*, but a celestial reward in eternity.' Richer students had separate rooms, refectory, and chapel. Their fees were devoted to the maintenance of the poor. Remembering his native as well as his adopted country, Standonk instituted similar colleges at Cambrai, Louvain, Mechlin, and Valenciennes, so that the College of Montaigu became the chief of an order. The peculiar dress of its students was a small cape or hood, from which they were called Capetians, a symbol of their poverty, and, like the garb of Charterhouse boys, exposing them to the gibes of wealthier scholars.

The noble aim of Standonk, like that of the religious orders, broke down through being carried to an extreme. Erasmus, a contemporary of Major at Montaigu, has left

Erasmus' satire on Montaigu.

a biting satire on it in his colloquy—of *Ichthyophagia*—
between a Salt-fishmonger and a Butcher, who complains of
want of custom from a college which ate no meat.

'About thirty years ago', says the Fishmonger, 'I lived
at the college called Vinegar College [i.e. *Mons Acetus*],' a
pun on Mons Acutus, or Montaigu.——*The Butcher*. ''That's
indeed a name of wisdom. Did a Salt-fishmonger live in that
sour college? No wonder he is so acute a student in divinity,
for I hear the very walls speak divinity.'—*The Fishmonger*.
'Yes, but as for me I brought nothing out of it, but
my body infected with the worst diseases, and the largest
quantity of the smallest animals. . . . What with lying hard,
bad diet, late and hard studies, within one year, of many young
men of a good genius some were killed, others driven mad,
others became lepers, some of whom I knew very well,
and, in short, not one but was in danger of his life.
Was not this cruelty against our neighbours? Neither was
this enough, but, adding a cowl and hood, he took away the
eating of flesh.' More follows to the same purpose. It is
easy to see the exaggeration, but Erasmus, too wise to rest in
exaggeration, closes with the remark: 'Nor do I mention these
things because I have any ill will to the college, but I thought
it worth while to give this warning lest human severity should
mar inexperienced and tender youth under the pretence of
religion. If I could but see that those that put on a cowl
put off naughtiness I should exhort everybody to wear one.
Besides, the spirit of vigorous youths is not to be cowed to
this sort of life, but the mind is rather to be educated to
piety.' Not less sensible are the remarks of Crévier, who
condemned Erasmus for want of moderation in his censures.
'The health of young men requires to be attended to, and it is
to attack it by two batteries to fatigue the spirit by study and
the body by a too severe regimen. The discipline of Standonk
has not been able to maintain itself. Besides mitigations

Ascetic discipline.

introduced by usage, it had to be softened by express rules.'
Yet it was still described by a German artist, who visited Paris
in 1654, as 'a stately college in which ill-bred boys [*ungerathene
Kinder*] are treated as if in a House of Correction. We were
not allowed to visit it with our sword, supposing it might be
used to set them free'[1].

Erasmus had the bodily infirmity which, as in a great chief
of our literature lately lost, too often accompanies intellectual
power. He said of himself he had a Protestant stomach, but
a Catholic soul. A Protestant who has rarely dined in his life
without meat can scarcely realise what a bad fish and vegetable
diet, broken only by frequent total fasts, must have been.
Major, who probably heard the taunts of Erasmus before they [Major's encomium on Montaigu.]
found a place in in his *Colloquies*, takes frequent occasion to
refer to Montaigu College in a different spirit, calling it 'an
illustrious museum', 'a frugal, but not ignoble house', 'the
nurse of his studies, never to be named without reverence'.
Yet he seems himself to have suffered from the hard life,
for he mentions, in the dedication of the *Parva Logicalia*, a
fever which had nearly cost him his life. He had doubtless
seen many of his contemporaries and pupils, besides David
Cranstoun, carried to the Graveyard of Poor Students, which
lay opposite the College gate.

To the Scottish father in the end of the fifteenth century,
inquiring to what college shall I send my son, or to the youth
left to shift for himself with scanty purse, these hardships
were too distant to be thought of. The College of Montaigu [Scottish students at Montaigu.]
offered the double attraction of economy and fame. Hither,
besides many forgotten names, came, during the time of Major's
connection with it, George Dundas from Lothian, a learned
Greek and Latin scholar, afterwards Preceptor of the Knights
of St. John in Scotland ; Hector Boece, the historian, from
Dundee, who praises Standonk as an exemplar of all the virtues ;

[1] *Topographia Galliæ*, by Martin Zeiller ; Frankfort, 1655.

and three other Angus men: Patrick Panther, who became secretary to James IV., writer of most of the Epistolæ Regum Scotorum in James IV.'s and part of James V.'s reign; Walter Ogilvy, celebrated for his eloquent style, and William Hay, schoolfellow of Boece at Dundee, afterwards his colleague and successor in the King's College of Aberdeen [1]. Here too were four countrymen of Major from East Lothian: George Hepburn[2], of the house of Hailes, Abbot of Arbroath, afterwards Bishop of the Isles, who fell at Flodden; Robert Walterson[3], a co-regent; David Cranstoun[4] and Ninian Hume, his pupils. Cranstoun dying young, but already distinguished, left his property to the College; the other was one of Major's favourite students. In Paris, possibly at Montaigu, as we learn for the first time from one of Major's prefaces, at the same period studied Gavin Douglas, Bishop of Dunkeld, whose chequered ecclesiastical and brilliant literary career gained him a prominent place in the history as well as the literature of Scotland; and Robert Cockburn, a Haddington man, afterwards Bishop of Ross[5], and Gavin Dunbar[6], afterwards Archbishop of Glasgow, whose studies in philosophy at Paris, and in the civil and canon law at Angers, overlooked by his biographers, are commemorated in Major's dedication of his Commentary on St. Luke.

The number of Scottish students at Paris during the time of Major's residence must have been very considerable, though it is impossible to give an exact estimate. The German Nation, the name substituted for the English Nation in 1378, after the withdrawal of the English, had been originally divided into three tribes: Germania Superior, Germania

---

[1] Hector Boece: *Aberdonensium Episcoporum Vitae*, p. 60.

[2] Uncle of first Earl of Bothwell. See Keith: *Scottish Bishops*, p. 174.

[3] Provost of Bothanis and Rector of Petcokkis, grants a charter of lands in Haddington to support a chaplain at the church of the Holy Trinity at Haddington.—*Great Seal Reg.*, 8th April 1539, No. 1902.

[4] Michel: *Les Ecossais en France*, ii. p. 324. See Appendix I. p. 412: Bibliography of D. Cranstoun.

[5] Bishop 1508-21.—Keith, p. 42.   [6] Archbishop 1524-47.—Keith, p. 521.

LIFE OF JOHN MAJOR

Inferior, and Scotia, which included the Irish and the few English who remained, continued to be the name of the third till 1528, when the tribes were reduced to two: the *Continentales* and the *Insulani*, perhaps a concession to the dislike of the English to be classed under Scotia when the relations between England and France had somewhat improved.

Besides the more celebrated of his countrymen already mentioned, we find references in Major's prefaces to Hugo Spens, his predecessor as Principal of St. Salvator's; Gavin Logy, Rector of St. Leonard's; John Forman, Precentor of Glasgow[1], a kinsman of the archbishop of that name; Peter Chaplain[2], Rector of Dunino, and Peter Sandilands[3], Rector of Calder; Robert Caubraith[4], George Turnbull[5], friends of Ninian Hume,—so, probably, like him, Lothian men; George Lockhart[6] from Ayrshire; Robert Bannerman, Thomas Ramsay[7], William Guynd, and John Annand. The list might be much enlarged from the Accounts of the German Nation from 1494 to 1530, fortunately preserved in the archives of the University, and still extant in the library of the Sorbonne[8]. In the year 1494, when Major

Other Scotsmen in Paris.

---

[1] Protocol Book of Cuthbert Simon, *Grampian Club*, pp. 285, 478, 480, 484, 485, 486.

[2] Canon of St. Salvator and Rector of Dunino.—*Great Seal Reg.* 1513-46, Index, p. 803; *ibidem*, Nos. 354, 2168, 2605.

[3] Hector Boece in *Aberdonensium Episcoporum Vitae*, p. 58, mentions amongst the Professors at St. Andrews, Wilhelmum Guyndum, Johannem Annandiae, ' viros spectatae doctrinae qui tametsi hactenus magisterii in theologia renuerunt fastigium de se modestius sentientes doctoribus tamen eos nemo dixerit eruditione inferiores.' Annand was the first Professor in Arts (in re literaria) of St. Leonard's, *ib.* p. 59.

[4] Robert Caubraith, a pupil of Major, and author of several works on Logic, described by Prantl, iv. p. 257, may perhaps be Robert Galbraith, Rector of Spot in 1534.—*Great Seal Reg.*, No. 1332.

[5] George Turnbull may perhaps be the Rector of Largo of that name.—*Great Seal Reg.* 1517, No. 1355.

[6] George Lockhart, a pupil of Major, wrote several works on Logic, described in the Bibliographical Appendix, *infra*, p. 414.

[7] Canon of St. Salvator, and Rector of Kemback 1517.—*Great Seal Reg.*, No. 175.

[8] Charles Jourdain's *Excursions Historiques à travers le Moyen Age*, 1888: ' Un Compte de la Nation d'Allemagne au xve siècle.'

passed as licentiate, of twenty-nine fellow-graduates eleven were Scotchmen, besides eight bachelors. His election as Quaestor or Receiver of this Nation in 1501 is proof that he possessed the confidence of his fellow-students, and the passages from the Prefaces to his works printed in the Appendix show that many of them, not only his own compatriots, but Frenchmen, Belgians, and Spaniards, were his warm admirers and personal friends. Seldom has the contemporary fame of a Professor risen higher or spread wider.

The value of oatmeal diet.

Of his favourite and most distinguished pupil David Cranstoun Major tells a significant anecdote[1]. When in his first course of theology, two fellow-students, Jacobus Almain of Sens[2] and Peter of Brussels[3], of the order of Friar Preachers, twitted him in the court of the Sorbonne, on the day of the divinity lecture, before his comrades, that the commons in Scotland eat oatmeal, as they had heard from a friar who had travelled there. They wished, says Major, to try a man whose quick temper they knew, by this jest which was really honourable to his country; but he attempted to deny it as a discredit. We understand, indeed, he adds, 'that a Frenchman coming from Britain brought home with him some of these cakes [panes] as curiosities [monstra]'. He then describes with singular accuracy and evident pride the mode of making them, and recals Froissart's[4] statement that the Scotch, both nobles and commons, used them in their campaigns, as if to say (for he leaves deductions to his readers),—'Let Frenchmen and

---

[1] *Hist.* 1. ii. p. 10.

[2] Almain's works on Logic, described by Prantl, iv. p. 238, appear to be lost, but his Theological Dissertation against Cardinal Caietan, and in favour of the authority of Councils as superior to that of the Pope, is preserved, p. lviii.

[3] Peter of Brussels wrote *Quaestiones* on the Organon of Aristotle, a *Commentary* on Peter the Spaniard, and *Quodlibeta.*—Prantl, iv. p. 275. He died 1511. On the title-page of his *Quaestiones*, published after his death in 1514, he is described as 'a most strenuous defender and interpreter of Thomas Aquinas'. He was regarded as a lost sheep recovered for the fold of the Thomists.

[4] Froissart, ii. 19.

Englishmen laugh, my countrymen have won battles on this fare'. Froissart might almost have been the Frenchman who brought home the oatcakes, so keenly does he seem to have been struck by the poverty of the Scots. 'When the barownes and knightes of Fraunce, who were wonte to fynde fayre hostelryes, halles hanged, and goodly castelles, and softe beddes to reste in, sawe themselfes in that necessite, they began to smyle, and said to the admyrall, Sir, what pleasure hath brought vs hyder? we neuer knewe what pouertie ment tyll nowe: we fynde nowe the old sayinge of our fathers and mothers true, whane they wolde saye, Go your waye, and ye lyue long, ye shall fynde harde and poore beddes, whiche nowe we fynde; therfore lette vs go oure voyage that we be come for; lette vs ryde into Englāde; the longe leivyenge here in Scotlande is to vs nother honourable nor profytable.'

To the youth of such a country the food of the College of Montaigu would not seem so poor as to Erasmus, a native of wealthy Rotterdam.

In 1499 Standonk, the second founder of Montaigu, was banished from Paris. He had quarrelled with Louis XII. as to the privileges of the students of the university, of which he was so strenuous an advocate that he advised a cessation of all studies, and even of the services in the churches, if they were infringed. He had touched the king in a still more delicate point, the divorce of Louis from Jane of France, the daughter of Louis XI., and his marriage to Anne of Brittany, widow of Charles VIII., his half-brother. It was very likely in consequence of this banishment of Standonk, and the royal displeasure with the College of Montaigu, that Major became affiliated to the College of Navarre, from which he got the income of a fellowship[1] and the post of theological professor, but he continued to act as regent in Montaigu, where he had taken his degree in arts, which entitled him to teach, and did

Major lectures at Navarre College.

---
[1] Launoi: *Historia*, p. 598.

His Spanish students.

not avail himself of his right to migrate to Navarre. The substance of his lectures on Logic, printed before in separate parts, was collected in 1508 in one volume, printed at Lyons, and dedicated to his pupil Ninian Hume. In the dedication he mentions that he had been urged by Louis Coronel, his brother Antony[1], and Gaspar Lax[2], three Spanish students, to print his commentaries on the *Summulae* of their countryman, Peter the Spaniard. They pleaded that as he had given some of his lectures on logic to his countryman David Cranstoun, James Almain of Sens, Peter Crockaert of Brussels, and Robert Senalis of Paris[3], they had equal reason to ask for a similar favour. But he urges reasons on the other side (for even the preface of a schoolman must be argumentative): his own inertia, the severe criticism of works of living authors, and his change of vocation to that of the study of the Sentences of Peter Lombard. He had always been willing to lecture slowly, that whoever wished might commit his lectures to writing. 'It is natural, however', he continues, 'that I should publish at large and distinctly what they wrote down from memory after dinner and supper. If I had imagined my lectures would have circulated so widely, I would have bestowed greater pains on them. But I did not know how to recall them, and since they were much sought after at the booksellers', I should at least have ploughed my own ground so far as my poor abilities allowed. It is easy', he concludes, 'to get angry. Unlearned as well as learned write poems everywhere. I dedicate these lectures to you both on account of your noble birth and your diligence in the knotty points of dialectic—knowing you will accept this little book, though unworthy of you, out of regard for the good-will of the author. Robert Walterson of

---

[1] The author of many Logical Treatises.—Prantl, iv. p. 53.
[2] Gaspar Lax, of Aragon, also a writer on Logic.—Prantl, iv. p. 255.
[3] The *Exponibilia*, his first printed work in Paris, 1503 (Bibliography, No. 1); the Commentaries on Peter the Spaniard at Lyons in 1505 (No. 2); other Logical Tracts at Paris in 1506 (No. 5).

Haddington, a co-regent with me in Montaigu, and our friend John Zacharias, beg to be remembered to you. Farewell.'

A letter from Louis Coronel[1] to his brother Antony is annexed, written in the enthusiastic vein of a young disciple overflowing with praise of the learning of Paris, 'whose streams flow to the remotest nations, and whose purest water springs from Mons Acutus, "the Hill of God", a rich mountain in which it pleaseth him to dwell, for the words of the Psalmist may without absurdity be applied to it—whose founder was Standonk, whom God has taken to himself[2], and where our master, John Major, lectured, whose learning will commend him not only to posterity but to eternity'. His small part has been, he modestly says, to revise the press and add a table of contents, which he dedicates to his brother in studies as in kin. In similar, even more high-flown, language Robert Senalis compared Montaigu to Parnassus, the Mons Sacer of Ovid, ' changing Sacer into Acer, in spite of the false quantity, to correspond to the French name of Montaigu', the philosophy taught there to the fountain of Hippocrene—

Louis Coronel's encomium on Major.

'Fons nitet in medio vitreis argenteus undis
Gregorius celeri quem pede ferit equus—

and Major himself to 'the Gregorian horse Pegasus', for 'its Pegasus', he says, 'is that incomparable master in Arts and Philosophy, my Professor, whom I cannot praise as much as he deserves, John Major, who flies on his own wings higher than the clouds would carry him, till he passes above all spirits in sublimity'.[3]

The treatise or lectures of Major on Logic are in the style which might be almost called stereotyped of mediæval scholas-

Major's Lectures on Logic.

---

[1] Louis Coronel of Segovia was less famous than his brother Antony, who wrote several works on Logic in which he followed Major.—Prantl, iv. 252. Both brothers were pupils of Major. Antony edited and concluded Major's *Libri Consequentiarum*; see p. 28.

[2] Standonk died 1501.

[3] 'Roberti Senalis Oratio': Paris, 1510.

tics. He commences with the special proposition or thesis
'Whether complex terms should be used'[1], as a sort of prelude
or introduction, and then comments in short almost shorthand
tracts on various points of Logic. This is followed by two
books on Terms and a tractate on the Liber Summularum of
Petrus Hispanus[2], which forms the chief part of the book.
Discussions are appended on the Predicables with the tree of
Porphyry; on the Predicaments; on Syllogisms; on Places [de
Locis]; on Fallacies; on matters which can be explained and
those which are insoluble; a small tract entitled, after the
example of Aristotle, Libri Posteriores; and another, Libri Consequentiarum, begun by Major but concluded by Antony Coronel.
In the same volume is continued a treatise on Parva Logicalia,
probably a separate course of lectures, with a fresh dedication
to Ninian Hume. The whole is concluded with a discussion
of a proposition or thesis 'On the Infinite', and one of the
Dialogues of which Major, like other Schoolmen, was so fond,
entitled 'Trilogus inter duos logicos et magistrum'.

College of Navarre.

The College of Navarre which hospitably adopted the celebrated Scottish Regent was in all respects a contrast to
Montaigu. A Royal College founded in 1305 by Jeanne of
Navarre, the wife of Philip the Fair, it had continued to
receive endowments from sovereigns and nobles, and was the
richest, perhaps the only very rich, college in a university where
poverty, although not the extreme poverty of Montaigu, was
the rule. It had twenty bursars in grammar, thirty in logic, and
twenty in divinity, and secured the ablest teachers. Its church
was used by the French Nation and for university sermons, which
gave it a certain precedence. It had the custody of the university archives and a splendid library. A reform of the fifteenth

---

[1] *De complexo significabili.* A fuller list of the contents of Major's Logical Lectures is given in the Bibliography, and an explanation of some of the terms used, in Appendix to Life, II. p. 94.

[2] Peter the Spaniard, who became Pope John XXI., and whose *Summulæ* were the text-book of Logic as the *Sentences* of Peter the Lombard, Bishop of Paris, were of Divinity.

century made it a college 'de plein exercice', with a full curriculum in Arts, in which Logic as well as Grammar and Rhetoric were taught. It had even retained two courses in Theology, which the Sorbonne tried to absorb to the exclusion of other colleges. But its chief fame was due to an illustrious succession of students and doctors. Launoi, himself a fellow in the seventeenth century, wrote an elaborate and admirable history of Navarre, which includes lives of 'its host of celebrated men'. Room is still found in the Annals of Learning in the fourteenth century for Nicholas Oresme, one of its masters, a political economist, a Greek scholar, and a mathematician, and Nicholas Clemangis, the theologian; in the fifteenth, for Peter D'Ailly, bishop of Cambray, and John Gerson, 'the most Christian Doctor', and in the sixteenth, for Budaeus, the friend and rival of Erasmus in the revival of the study of the classical languages. To Launoi's work we owe the most authentic record of Major's career in Paris, for Major also was deemed one of the chief luminaries of Navarre. D'Ailly and Gerson, successively Chancellors of the University as well as Principals of Navarre, led the famous movement for reform within the church which asserted itself in the beginning of the fifteenth century, at the Councils of Pisa (1409) and Constance (1414-18). They were the principal authors or authorities in favour of the supremacy of General Councils over the Pope, the early champions of the Gallican Liberties, who after so many gallant struggles were only finally defeated by the Ultramontane doctrine of Papal Infallibility established as *de fide* by the Vatican Council of the present century. Colleges like nations have traditions, and the connection of Major with Navarre, where Gerson's name still exercised great influence, favoured his adoption of the Gallican position that the Pope was not the ultimate authority when opposed by a General Council. His views on this point, carried to lengths from which Major himself would have shrunk, by his pupils Knox and Buchanan, form a link in the chain of opinion which produced the Reformation.

Famous Scholars of Navarre.

A special opportunity arose during Major's residence in Paris of reasserting Gallican doctrines.

The policy which led Charles VIII. and Louis XII. to claim parts of Italy, and to assert their claim by the sword, brought the latter monarch into conflict with Julius II., the strenuous maintainer of the temporal rights and spiritual supremacy of the Papacy. In the course of this conflict Louis tried the bold stroke of calling a Council to overrule the Pope. The Council of Pisa met in 1511, was adjourned to Milan and finally to Lyons, but owing to the failure of Louis's Italian campaign accomplished nothing. During its sittings Cardinal Thomas Cajetan published a book on the papal side, impugning its authority, and Louis applied to the University of Paris to answer it. The task was intrusted to James Almain, a young Master of Arts and member of the College of Navarre, one of Major's pupils. This *Liber de Auctoritate Ecclesiæ et Conciliorum adversum Thomam Caietanum* has been sometimes credited to Major as joint author, but Launoi, our best authority, ignores this. Almain probably sought his advice, and Major we may be certain was present in the crowded auditory of approving theologians when it was publicly read at Paris. The treatise of Almain supported views quite in accordance with the teaching of his master. In the later edition of the works of Gerson[1] there is inserted an appendix 'Doctoris Majoris Doctoris Parisiensis Disputationes de Statu ac Potestate Ecclesiæ excerptæ ad verbum ex ejusdem Commentariis in Librum Quartum Sententiarum'. This appendix contains arguments proving (1) That the polity of the church is monarchical or constitutional (as we now say) as distinguished from absolute; (2) *That Bishops and Parish Priests were both directly instituted by Christ* (a step in the direction of Presbyterian equality); and (3) That the Pope has not the power of the sword over Christian Kings and

Navarre supports Gallican doctrines.

---

[1] *Opera Gersoni*; Antw. ed. 1760, vol. ii. pp. 1121, 1131, 1145.

Princes; also Disputations on the Authority of the Council over the Pope and of the Power of the Pope in Temporal Affairs. These latter disputations consist of extracts from Major's later work, 'A Commentary on Matthew', and show that he gave a wide scope to the idea of a commentary in order to introduce opinions he desired to promulgate.

In 1505-6 Major graduated as Doctor in Theology, and as by a rule of the College of Navarre Professors in Arts were obliged to leave off lecturing in that Faculty after attaining this degree, then or soon after he transferred his services to the Theological Faculty, and, still living in Montaigu, commenced to lecture in the Sorbonne on the Sentences of Peter Lombard, the recognised text-book of the theological school.

1505-6 Major a Doctor of Theology.

The Sorbonne had different traditions from Navarre, and was the head and centre of Roman orthodoxy. It is perhaps not altogether fanciful to see in the balancing character of his mind some traces of the influence of schools which represented opposite tendencies—Reform and Conservatism, Independence and Authority. A more ancient foundation of the middle of the thirteenth century, the Sorbonne had been instituted and organised by Robert de Sorbonne, chaplain of St. Louis, as a college for secular priests and the cultivation of theology. Its endowments and its numbers were small. It had only thirty fellows (*socii*) and commoners (*hospites*), the former always in orders and bachelors and doctors in theology, the latter, bachelors of the same faculty. But the small numbers and the strictness of the rules as to election of fellows gave the Doctors of the Sorbonne a distinction, and in process of time—especially at epochs when doctrinal questions became prominent—an authority, which led to their being recognised as a necessary constituent part of the divinity faculty, and to the gradual suppression of theological teaching in other colleges. The influence of

The Sorbonne.

the Sorbonne, which became as it were a Divinity Hall, was exercised against the new light shed upon theology by the study of the Scriptures in the original languages and affords a warning to those who would exile theology from the Universities. Before Major became one of the Doctors they had condemned the study of Greek and Hebrew as adverse to theology. Shortly after he returned to Scotland they set the example (immediately followed by Oxford and Cambridge) of burning the works of Luther. This act was the occasion of a violent tract by the mild Melanchthon,—' A Defence of Martin Luther against the furious decree of the Parisian Theologasters', in which Major came in for a share of the invective. 'I have seen', he says, 'the commentaries on Peter Lombard by John Major, a man, I am told, now the prince of the Paris Masters. What waggon-loads of trifles! What pages he fills with dispute whether horsemanship requires a horse, whether the sea was salt when God made it, not to speak of the many lies he has written about the freedom of the will, not only in the teeth of the Scriptures, but of all the schoolmen. If he is a specimen of the Paris Doctors, no wonder they are little favourable to Luther.'[1]

Sorbonnic style.

To the Sorbonne, besides graver defects of the scholastic theology, Major is said to have owed his singularly cramped Latin. A Sorbonnic style was a nickname for the style opposed to the easier and better form of composition which the study of the ancient classics and the use of the vulgar tongues introduced. Yet Latin at best was now an old-fashioned garb, worn with grace by scholars like Erasmus, Buchanan, Scaliger, but to inferior genius or the ordinary man a rigid uniform which constrained the free play of the mind. Every one must regret that Major's like Buchanan's history was not written, as Bellenden's translation of Boece was, in the dialect of their native country, which both knew so well. They might

---

[1] Melanchthonii *Opera*, i. p. 398.

possibly have preserved for a time Scottish prose, as Dunbar and Douglas preserved Scottish poetry, to the enrichment of the future language and literature of Britain.

Four years after his theological degree an attempt was made by his friend Gavin Douglas to recall Major to Scotland[1]. In 1509 a precept passed the Privy Seal at the instance of Douglas for his presentation to the office of Treasurer of the Chapel Royal, then vacant. But for some reason, probably Major's unwillingness to quit the duties of a teacher, which he preferred to those of ecclesiastical office, the project fell through. It would appear, however, from a passage in his Commentary on the Fourth Book of the Sentences, that Major did revisit Scotland in 1515. The passage referred to first appears in the edition of 1519[2], and in it he states that when he had been at home four years before and visited the Monastery of Melrose, he was told of a frequent custom of the Abbots to let their rich pastures with the sheep to tenants on condition that they should be liable for loss of the stock—in other words, under the contract known in Scottish law as a Bowing Contract[3]. He adds that in answer to repeated inquiries he was told this custom had led to the pauperisation of the tenants or sheep-masters, who had formerly lived like wealthy patriarchs. It is enough, he concludes, to show the iniquity of such contracts. The passage is curious as evidence how keenly the Doctor of Theology still watched the rural pursuits in which he had probably spent his boyhood. It is a warning also, in the meagreness of our information as to the details of his life, against the assumption that he may not have more than once returned to Scotland during his Paris residence. It was but a short voyage of about a week, with favourable weather, from

Major visits Scotland, 1515.

---

[1] *Memoir of Gavin Douglas*, by John Small, Librarian of the University of Edinburgh, prefixed to edition of his works.
[2] Dist. xv., Qu. 46, fol. clxiii.
[3] See Hunter, *Landlord and Tenant*, i. 344. This anomalous form of Lease is now confined to dairy farms, and as to its local limits.—Rankine, *Leases*, p. 255.

Calais or Dieppe to the English or Scottish east coast ports, yet had it not been for this solitary and casual reference, we should not have known that Major ever came back to Scotland till his return in 1518, the occasion of which will be noticed presently.

Theological Studies. Peter Lombard. His first published work on theology was his *Commentary on the 4th Book of Peter the Lombard's Sentences*, issued in 1509. This was followed by his Commentary on the First and Second Books in 1510, and on the Third in 1517. The popularity of these Commentaries was shown by new editions of the Fourth Book in 1512, 1516, 1519, and 1521, of the First in 1519 and 1530, of the Second in 1519 and 1528, and of the Third in 1528.

Nor was the scholastic and philosophical activity of Major confined to the publication of his own works. He edited in 1505, along with a Spaniard, Magister Ortiz[1], the Medulla, or Essence of Logic, by Jerome Pardus[2]; in 1510 a short tract of Buridan[3]; in 1512 the epitome, by Adam Godham[4], of the four Books of the Sentences, as abridged by Henry Van Oyta[5], a Viennese doctor of the end of the 14th century; and in 1517 he suggested to two of his pupils and superintended the first issue of the *Reportata Parisiensia* of his famous countryman[6] John Duns Scotus. Ockham was the pupil of Duns Scotus. Buridan and Godham were pupils of Ockham[7]. Three cer-

---

[1] Ortiz, at first an opponent in Paris, afterwards a patron in Spain, of Ignatius Loyola, was one of Charles v.'s agents in Rome in the case of Queeen Katharine. The biographer of Ignatius states that when Ortiz broke down under the strain of the spiritual exercises at Monte Cassino, St. Ignatius, to cheer his friend, danced for him the old national dance of the Basques. It cheered him so that he was roused from his stupor and finished his exercises.—Stewart Rose, *Ignatius Loyola*, p. 123. Many of his despatches from Rome, with reference to the Divorce, are in the Calendars of State Papers, Rolls Series. He is called by Mr. Froude ' a bitter Catholic theologian, with the qualities of his profession.'— *The Divorce*, p. 159.

[2] The contents of the *Medulla* are described by Prantl, iv. p. 246.

[3] John Buridan (*ob. c.* 1358), a voluminous writer on Logic and Metaphysics, whose works are described by Prantl, iv. p. 14.

[4] See his Life in *Dict. of Nat. Biography*.

[5] A Viennese writer on Theology as well as Logic (*ob.* 1397).—Prantl, iv. p. 103.

[6] *History*, IV. xvi. p. 207.   [7] *History*, IV. xxi. p. 230.

tainly, perhaps all, of these writers were Franciscans. Duns Scotus was the founder of the school which, taking his name, separated itself from the hitherto orthodox scholastic doctrine of Thomas Aquinas[1]. Ockham was the founder of the still more radical revolt of the Nominalists against the Realists[2]— and in this Godham[3] and Buridan[4] followed him. It eventually led, according to Hauréau, to the dissolution of the Scholastic Philosophy[5]. While Major is careful not to identify his own opinions with any of these authors, it is impossible to overlook the fact that he chose their writings for republication.

Major inclines to Nominalism.

In the singular conclusion of his life of Adam Godham, now for the first time reprinted[6], Major assigns the first place amongst the learned men of Britain to the Venerable Bede, the second to Alexander Hales, but he adds Ockham and Godham would have contended for it were not Hales so much their senior. These two he pronounces equal, and contrasts them in a passage which is a sample of his style and criticism

---

[1] Thomas Aquinas and Duns Scotus were both Realists. But Duns set the first great example of a breach in the unity of scholastic doctrine, so that Schwegler (*History of Philosophy*, Hutchison Stirling's translation, p. 145), even says: 'The whole foundation of scholastic metaphysics was abandoned the moment Duns Scotus transferred the problem of Theology to the practical sphere. With the separation of theory and practice, and still more with the separation in Nominalism of thought and thing, philosophy became divided from theology, reason from faith.'

[2] He is classed by the writer who has most exhaustively examined his writings as one of the Moderns, or of the school of Scotist Terminists. See Appendix to the Life, No. II.

[3] Godham, a somewhat obscure schoolman, whose name was sometimes spelt Woodham, is rated higher by Major than by the veterans of philosophy. He attended Ockham's lectures at Oxford, and died, 1358, at Norwich, where he was a member of the Franciscan Convent, or at Bubwell, near Bury.—*Dict. of Nat. Biography*, s.v. GODDAM; Prantl, ii. p. 6.

[4] John Buridan, who died shortly after Goddam, was a much more decided follower of their common master Ockham, and expressly declared the distinction between Metaphysics and Theology to be that the former recognised only what could be proved by reason, while the latter proceeded from certain dogmatic principles which it accepted without evidence, and reasoned from them.—Prantl, iv. p. 15. Buridan is perhaps now chiefly remembered by the fallacy of the Asinus Buridani, though the Ass is not to be found in his writings.

[5] *Philosophie Scholastique.*   [6] Appendix II. p. 431.

at their best. 'Ockham and Godham are equals in logic and in either kind of philosophy (Ethics and Metaphysics?). Ockham in commenting on the Sentences is wordy and diffuse. Godham is concise and firm; if Ockham's dialectic (dialogus) did not stand in the way, the younger writer would carry off the palm. Ockham's intellect was sublime and daring, Godham's noble and solid. The one with knitted brow, lowered eyebrows, and flashing eyes, as a warrior from youth, disputes with gravity. The other, with calm brow and raised eyebrows, laughingly pleases every one, and resolves everything (*diluit omnia*), so that I prefer neither.'

This balancing, hesitating, and inconclusive judgment is very characteristic of Major's intellect. Though he is positive enough in his opinions on individual points, and in resting finally on orthodox conclusions, many of his arguments were, it would be wrong to say sceptical[1], but as little dogmatic as was possible in a schoolman. It is also deserving of note that he praises 'the Dialogus of Ockham', for that work is described in his History as 'treating of many things concerning the Pope, and the Emperor, laying down nothing definitely, but leaving everything to the judgment of his audience'. This too was Major's method when he came to deal with ticklish points as to the Pope's authority. But if Major supposed he really left the question of the Pope's authority where he found it, he deceived himself. The tendency of his thoughts could not be concealed, and his doubts and questions were solved and answered by the younger generation's acts.

<small>Major attempts to reconcile Nominalism and Realism on Nominalist Principles.</small>

The exact position of Major amongst the scholastic philosophers is a subject which would require and repay a separate monograph. It is beyond the power of the present writer to

---

[1] Mr. Owen, in his *Evenings with the Skeptics*, Longmans, 1881, does not hesitate to class even the earlier schoolmen, Erigena, Abelard, Aquinas, as semi-Sceptics, but the tendency became more distinctly marked in William of Ockham and the Nominalists.

furnish it, and would exceed the limits of this sketch, as well as probably exhaust the patience of most of its readers[1]. Yet to leave it altogether untouched—to present any however imperfect a portrait of the last of the Scottish Schoolmen without some notice of his philosophical standpoint would be the play of Hamlet without Hamlet. Fortunately Major has himself, in a short passage of the Preface to the standard edition of his Commentary on the Fourth Book of the Sentences, published in 1519, given a clue to the aim of his philosophy. 'I have yet seen,' he writes, 'none of the Nominalists who has carried his work on the Fourth Book of the Sentences to the core and the close (*ad umbilicum et calcem*), and this others retort on them as an opprobrium, saying that the Nominalists are so occupied with Logic and Philosophy that they neglect Theology. And yet there are various subjects of Theology which presuppose Metaphysics. I will attempt therefore to apply the principles of the Nominalists to the several Distinctions of the Fourth Book of the Sentences, and to write one or more questions which the Realists too, if they pay attention, can easily understand. Either way, Theology, about which I shall specially treat, will be common ground.' Here again we find Major taking in the great controversy which divided the schools since the time of Ockham, and some have thought from a much earlier date, the position of a mediator, and endeavouring for the sake of Theology to reconcile Realism and Nominalism.

In 1518, having completed his work as lecturer on the Master of the Sentences, Major at last accepted the call his own country made on him to take part in its higher education. It is possible that his friend Gavin Douglas, now Bishop of Dunkeld, who revisited France in 1517 to negotiate the Treaty of Rouen, had renewed his entreaties with success. On 25th

---

[1] See further on Major's position as a Logician and Philosopher, Appendix to the Life, No. II. p. 94.

June 1518 Major was incorporated [1], before Adam Colquhoun, the Rector, as Principal Regent of the College and Paedagogium of Glasgow, and is described as Canon of the Chapel Royal at Stirling and Vicar of Dunlop, endowments no doubt bestowed on him to induce him to leave Paris, and which prove that he must have taken orders, though he devoted himself entirely to the educational side of the ministerial office.

In several passages of his writings he defends evidently with a personal reference the ecclesiastics who devoted themselves to philosophy and education in preference to pastoral duties. In one of these he says: 'Nor is there a reasonable ground for frequenting universities, except in so far as a man learns by attending lectures, so that he may return to his flock with greater learning. But if he is sufficiently instructed to be able to draw doctrine from books only, he can do that both in the flock committed to him and on Mount Caucasus, or the Rock of Parmenides. He too who continues to read theology in the university is equivalent to a preacher; nay more, he creates preachers, which is a greater work than to preach. He is most certainly excused if he has no cure of souls, and if he has simply received the order of the ministry. . . . If such a one, too, residing in a university, has a cure in the neighbourhood, it is not necessary that he should live in his parish, but it is sufficient if he have a good vicar to administer the Sacraments, provided he gives the food of life on festival days to his flock, and hears confessions and doubtful cases. For it is hard to say to a learned man, accustomed to live and converse with learned men, that he ought always to live in a country village. Truly it seems sufficient for him to dwell in the nearest town or city, and frequently to visit his parishioners, taking care that he is not absent on festival days unless for a reasonable cause'.[2]

---

[1] Register of Glasgow College.
[2] *In Quartum*, Dist. xxiv. Qu. 2, fol. clxvii.

LIFE OF JOHN MAJOR

In 1522 he is again named in the Glasgow Records as Professor of Theology and Treasurer of the Chapel Royal, as well as Vicar of Dunlop, and in 1523 he represented one of the Nations as elector (*intrans*) of the new Rector. On 9th June of the same year he migrated to St. Andrews, where he was incorporated under the titles of Theological Doctor of Paris and Treasurer of the Chapel Royal on the same day as Patrick Hamilton, the future martyr, who had studied under him in Glasgow. *[Regent in St. Andrews 1522.]*

Little record remains of Major's Glasgow period. He doubtless continued, perhaps repeated, his Paris lectures on Logic and Theology, and we find his name occurring in connection with the election of Rector and other College business. He was present at a congregation in 1522, when the Rector, James Stewart, protested against a tax being imposed on the University [1]. He is styled throughout the entries of the University Records, where his name occurs, 'Principalis Regens Collegii et Paedagogii', but the principal Regent in the old constitution of Glasgow was only the senior Professor, and the office of Principal in the modern sense did not then exist.

The whole of his residence in Glasgow was less than five years, but it would be memorable, if for no other reason, for one of his pupils. John Knox, a Haddington boy, had a link with Major, whose strong local feeling we have seen, and Major may have been the cause that, instead of going to St. Andrews, Knox matriculated at Glasgow in 1522. Unfortunately the Glasgow period of Knox's education is the barest in material of any part of his life. The future Reformer appears to have quitted the University without a degree, and his practical intellect led to his commencing life neither as a philosopher nor a theologian, but as a church notary [2]. His mind was of the quality which matures late, but often pro- *[John Knox one of his pupils at Glasgow.]*

---

[1] Munimenta Universitatis Glasguensis, p. 143.
[2] Memoir of John Knox, *Dictionary of National Biography*.

duces the strongest fruit. The only reference he makes to
Major belongs to a later period, when they were both at St.
Andrews, in a passage in which he describes his old master as
'a man whose word was reckoned an oracle in matters of
religion', proving that Major retained his previous reputation.

Glasgow in Major's time.

Glasgow was at the time Major lived in it a small but
beautiful city, situated on a fine river, not yet deepened by
art so as to be a channel of commerce. It was chiefly known
as the See of the great bishopric founded by Kentigern,
restored by David I. when Prince of Cumberland, and recently
raised to the dignity of an archbishopric, which embraced the
south-west and parts of the south of Scotland. The University
founded in the middle of the previous century had been poorly
endowed, and did not become celebrated till its reform by
Andrew Melville after the Reformation.

The Archbishop during Major's residence was James Beaton,
uncle of the more famous Cardinal; and the translation of
James to the See of St. Andrews in 1523 synchronises so well
with Major's removal to the elder and then more distinguished
University, that we can scarcely err in supposing that the one
promotion led to the other.

Major at St. Andrews.

If Edinburgh or Glasgow was a contrast to Paris, much
more was St. Andrews. By nature, the site now so venerable
between the sands at the mouth of the Eden and the rock-
bound coast at one of the extremities of the little realm of
Scotland, seemed destined for a fishing village or haven for
small craft which already in considerable numbers dared the
stormy sea and brought their native land in contact with the
civilisation of Europe. But towns did not rank then by size or
even by wealth. St. Andrews had a threefold dignity in the
eyes of the pious Catholic and the ecclesiastical scholar. It
held the relics of the patron Saint of Scotland. It was the
primatial See. It was the first, and still, notwithstanding
the foundation of Glasgow and Aberdeen, the principal Uni-

versity. The Bulls for its foundation had been obtained by
Bishop Wardlaw in 1411, tutor and friend of James I., who
confirmed the privileges granted to it in 1432. Bishop
Kennedy had founded the first College of St. Salvator in 1456,
and ten years before Major's incorporation St. Leonard's,
or the New College, had been endowed by Archbishop Stewart,
the bastard of James IV., and Prior John Hepburn. St. Salvator was instituted as a College for Theology and the Arts,
for divine worship combined with scholastic exercises. Its
members were a Provost, who was to be a Master or Doctor
in Theology, a Licentiate and a Bachelor of the same Faculty,
four Masters of Arts, and six poor Clerks.

St. Leonard's was modelled after the college for poor scholars
at Louvain, itself a copy of Montaigu College. Its foundation
consisted of a Principal and four Chaplains, two of them
Regents, and twenty Poor Scholars, instructed in the Gregorian
chant, and six of them Students of Theology. Its statutes,
drawn by Prior Hepburn, were of the strictest kind as regards
discipline, and the richer students, not on the foundation,
were to be obliged to conform to them. The scholars were to
be admitted on examination: not older than twenty-one, poor,
virtuous, versed in the first and second parts of grammar, good
writers, and good singers. The subjects prescribed for lectures
were grammar, poetry, and rhetoric, logic, physics, philosophy,
metaphysics, and one of the books of Solomon. It does not
appear that Major, when he came to St. Andrews, was at
first specially attached to either College, and as lectures continued in the Paedagogium, which Beaton converted into the
College of St. Mary in 1537, it is not possible to say where his
lectures were delivered; but he continued to teach according to
the same methods the same subjects as in Paris and Glasgow
—Logic and Theology.

In 1523, 1524, and 1525, he was elected one of the Dean's *Offices held by Major at St. Andrews.*
Assessors in the Faculty of Arts. In 1523 and 1525 he

was one of the deputies appointed to visit St. Salvator. In 1524 he was one of the Auditors of the Quæstor's accounts, and also one of the Rector's Assessors. The last date at which his name appears at this period was on 22d January 1525. It re-appears after an interval of nearly six years on 6th November 1531, when he was again elected one of the Deans, probably of the Faculty of Theology.

During his residence at Glasgow and St. Andrews it appears probable that Major paid special attention to the philosophical, and in particular the logical studies he had relinquished for a time in Paris, but now resumed for the sake of his own countrymen in the smaller universities of Scotland, which were, as they have always been, undermanned, and could not afford in that age separate professors even for philosophy and divinity. This would account for his Introduction to the Dialectic and whole Logic of Aristotle, a new and recent edition of his earlier work, digested in twelve books, which was issued by Badius Ascensius in Paris, while he was still absent in 1521, and the 'Eight Books of Physics with Natural Philosophy and Metaphysics,' published in 1526, shortly after his return, by Giles Gourmont, famous as a printer of Greek, and soon followed by his Logical Questions, issued from the same press in 1528. He finished his Aristotelian studies by the issue of a Treatise on the Ethics, published by Badius in 1530. He had thus, with a rare completeness, embraced in his Lectures and Works almost the whole range of the Aristotelian Philosophy. When we remember that an edition of a single work of Aristotle, or a single classic author, has been deemed sufficient for the labours and the fame of a modern university professor, we appreciate the indefatigable industry of Major, and we learn how little the nineteenth century can afford to despise the sixteenth in the matter of philosophical erudition.

Nor were these treatises of Major mere editions or commentaries on Aristotle. He reproduced and reduced in them

Completion of his study of Aristotle.

the substance of the thoughts of the great master to the scholastic method. So they were the effort and the fruit of independent thought. The scholastic method was then becoming antiquated, and was alien to the modern spirit. While it addressed itself to the highest problems which the human mind can attempt to solve or pronounce insoluble—the nature of God, the origin of man and the universe, the being and working of the mind itself—it descended also to the most trivial details, and put the most casuistical questions, which the sarcasm of Melanchthon, the satire of Rabelais, and the epigram of Buchanan could hardly exaggerate.

Still Major's work, always acutely critical and argumentative, was at least an educational discipline. It awakened and stimulated thought, perhaps the greatest service any teacher can render to his pupils. It is not surprising that one class of them learnt to swear by their master as an oracle, and another to criticise his method and despise its results.

In 1525 he returned to Paris and the College of Montaigu, probably to escape the troubles of the times. The earl of Angus was then at the head of affairs, and Major's patron, Beaton, had to hide himself in the disguise of a shepherd. Major probably also was glad of the opportunity his return afforded to superintend the publication of his Exposition of the Four Evangelists, which was issued from the press of Jodocus Badius Ascensius in 1529. His absence saved him from being a spectator of, probably an actor in, the trial of Patrick Hamilton, one of his Glasgow pupils, who was condemned for heresy by an Assembly of Bishops and Theologians at St. Andrews, and burnt before the gate of St. Salvator on 29th January 1528; but it was only to see a similar scene in the streets of Paris—the martyrdom of Berquin; for the decree of the Sorbonne in 1521 that 'flames rather than reasoning should be employed against the heresies of Luther' was applied to the Lutherans as well as their works. Amongst

Returns to Paris, 1525.

His Biblical Commentaries.

the doctrines for which Hamilton died were the assertions that it was lawful for all men to read the Word of God; that image-worship, and the Invocation of Saints and the Virgin, were unlawful; that masses for the dead were vain; that there was no such place as purgatory; that sin could be purged only by repentance and faith in the blood of Christ Jesus. There is no reason to suppose that Major would have dissented from the sentence any more than his master Gerson had from that against Huss. The Doctors of Louvain, who were in close sympathy with the Sorbonne, congratulated Beaton on having performed a commendable act, and Major's dedication of his *Commentary on St. Matthew* refers to the news recently received that Beaton had, 'not without the ill-will of many, manfully removed a person of noble birth, but an unhappy follower of the Lutheran heresy'. The allusion is an euphemistic reference to the martyrdom of Hamilton.

Major condemns Lutheran heresy.

To St. Andrews during Major's residence came a Highland youth, attracted by his fame, destined by nature for learning, already with some of the experience of a man. George[1], the son of Thomas Buchanan of the Moss, in Lennox, early lost his father, and was sent when fourteen, at the cost of his maternal uncle, James Heriot of Traprain, in East Lothian, to Paris; but after two years' study of the Latin classics the poverty of his mother brought him home, and he served with the French troops of Albany at the siege of Werk. The hardship of a winter camp led to an illness, and, after recruiting his health at home, he entered the Paedagogium at St. Andrews in 1524. On 3d October 1525 he took his degree of Bachelor of Arts. Major having gone to Paris in that year, Buchanan either accompanied or followed him, but entered, not as might have been expected the College of Montaigu, but the Scots College de Grisy, in which he was admitted *ad eundem* as Bachelor on

---

[1] A more favourable view of the character and conduct of George Buchanan will be found in Mr. P. Hume Brown's *Memoir*, 1890.

10th October 1527. There is no proof that Major was, as has been alleged, at the expense of his maintenance, but probably he befriended a young man connected with East Lothian as well as St. Andrews, whose talents foretold his future eminence. In 1529 Buchanan was elected Procurator of the German Nation, the highest honour then open to the Scottish student, having lost a prior election only through the superior claim of his blind countryman, Robert Wauchope, afterwards Bishop of Armagh. Buchanan has left two remarks on Major, in themselves not unfair, but very unjust if taken as a summary of his whole teaching. 'John Major at that time taught Dialectic, or rather Sophistic', he says, 'in extreme old age at St. Andrews'; and in the well-known epigram which associates their names, the pupil again expresses his repugnance for the scholastic triflings the younger generation found in works their elders deemed the glory of the University of Paris:— [George Buchanan.]

> Cum scateat nugis solo cognomine Major,
> Nec sit in immenso pagina sana libro,
> Non mirum titulis quod se veracibus ornat ;
> Nec semper mendax fingere Creta solet.

> When he proclaims himself thus clearly
> As 'Major' by cognomen merely,
> Since trifles through the book abound,
> And scarce a page of sense is found,
> Full credit sure the word acquires,
> For Cretans are not always liars !

The sting of the epigram is the last, not the first, line, which was taken from Major's description of himself on the title-page of more than one of his books[1]. Neither reverence nor gratitude were qualities of Buchanan, but the difference of age to a large extent accounts for his estimate of Major.

It would be difficult to imagine a greater contrast than the doctor of the Sorbonne trained at the feet of its masters, himself recognised as one of them, without poetic imagination, and [Contrast between Major and Buchanan.]

---

[1] See Appendices I. and II., pp. 430, 434, 435, 439.

with little experience of practical life except as seen from the cloister and the chair, and his young pupil already versed in the Latin Classics and the thoughts not of Thomas Aquinas and Duns Scotus, Peter the Spaniard and Peter the Lombard, but of Virgil, Horace, Catullus, and Martial, and who had seen not Paris merely but the Camp. A supercilious and unmeasured contempt for old-fashioned learning in a youth of genius has had examples before and since Buchanan. In truth Buchanan learnt more than he was conscious of from Major. The study of the sacred texts, the independent view of the sources of political authority, and the inclination towards exact historical inquiry, were notable points in Major's mental attitude, and can scarcely have failed to influence his students. The common opinion that the seeds of the *De Jure Regni*, and what are sometimes called the republican, but more accurately the constitutional, views of Buchanan's History were derived in part from Major's teaching, seems well founded. His position marks a stage through which the European mind had to pass before it abandoned scholasticism for humanism, the Roman for the Reformed doctrines, Absolute for Constitutional Government. The same Tendency has indeed been marked in earlier schoolmen by the historians of philosophy. What was special to the case of Major was that this Tendency was during his life coeval with the Renaissance Movement north of the Alps, and that while the Master resisted, his younger and active-minded disciples combined the necessary results of the union of the Tendency with the Movement.

Major's History, a copy of which, printed by Badius Ascensius in 1521, must have been in the St. Andrews Library, probably was known to the omnivorous student whose elaborate work, more than fifty years later[1], was to eclipse its fame.

The form of this History is unique. It is written in a scholastic style, and every now and then breaks out into logical

---

[1] The first edition of Buchanan's History was published by Alexander Arbuthnot at Edinburgh, 1582.

arguments. But what has been called in the nineteenth century the critical spirit, in the mode in which it manifested itself in the sixteenth century, is to be traced from the first page to the last. A renewed zeal for historical study was one of the features of the time. The age of the Monkish Chronicles and the Mediæval Annals was past. It was no longer possible to write history in the style of Matthew Paris and John of Fordun, or of Sir John Froissart, or even of Philip de Commines. With the advent of the new learning the historical instinct led all nations to desire a more exact account of their origin, and a more philosophical narrative of their progress, not merely stating events in the order of their occurrence, but tracing them to their causes. A series of historical works issued from the press of Badius about this period, in some of which there was more, in others less, of this instinct. The history of the kings of Britain by Geoffrey of Monmouth was published in 1508, the History of Scotland by Hector Boece in 1526, and that of Paulus Jovius, *De Rebus Gestis Francorum et Regum Franciae* in 1536,[1] besides some of the best old Chronicles, Saxo Grammaticus and Gregory of Tours. It was probably in contrast to Geoffrey of Monmouth's title to his History 'Britanniæ Utriusque regum et principum Origo et Gesta', that Major adopted the title of 'Historia *Majoris Britanniæ*'. *Scholastic form and critical spirit of his History.*

The lively and inquisitive Italian, Polydore Vergil, who had been sent in 1504 to collect Peter's Pence in England, was specially attracted to the early annals of Britain, and wrote in 1509 to James IV. for information as to the succession of the Scottish kings, but the information does not seem to have been supplied. Shortly before the death of Gavin Douglas in 1523 he met that prelate in London, and resumed his inquiries. Their conversation is typical of the contest going on in many minds between the old traditional and the new critical view of *Polydore Vergil and Gavin Douglas.*

---

[1] The *Compendium super Francorum Gestis*, by Robert Gaguin, published in 1497, appears to have been well known to Major, and is written more in his spirit than any of the other Histories of his time.

history. It is interesting too as showing that the Bishop's education in history had not advanced so far as that of his old friend Major the theologian, although there is some reason to believe that in theology the opposite was the case, and that Douglas leant more than Major towards the doctrines of the Reformation. This is a not uncommon phenomenon. The critical part of the intellect applies or confines itself to different departments in different minds. Douglas, according to Vergil, asked him 'not to follow the account recently published by a certain Scot which treats as a fable the descent of the Scottish kings from Gathelus, the son of an Athenian king, and Scota, the daughter of Pharaoh', and furnished him with the usual fictitious pedigree to prove it. The Scot was beyond doubt Major, whose History had been published two years before. Polydore was, like Major, incredulous. 'When I read the notes of Douglas', he says, 'according to the fable I seemed to see the bear bring forth her young. Afterwards when we met, as we were accustomed, this Gavin asked my opinion', and Polydore then argued, from the silence of the Roman historians, that there could have been no Picts or Scots in Britain prior to the Roman conquest, and, he adds: 'This Gavin, no doubt a sincere man, did the less dissent from this sentence, in that it plainly appeared to him that reason and truth herein well agreed, so easily is truth discovered from feigned phrases'. The death of Douglas by the plague prevented Polydore from further enjoying the benefit of his conversation.

The History of Major was entitled *Historia Majoris Britanniae tam Angliae quam Scotiae per Johannem Majorem natione quidem Scotum professione autem theologum.*

Title of Major's History.

'Major Britain' was no doubt, in its first intention, meant to distinguish Britain from Brittany, the lesser land of the Britons, just as Scotland, 'Scotia Minor', in mediæval Latin, prior to the eleventh century, was distinguished from Ireland, the 'Scotia Major' of the Scottish race. But it signified the author's presage of the greatness of the small island whose annals he relates. There is possibly too a play on his own name. It was Major's History of Major Britain. It was also an early essay to find a name that, without offence to the pride of either nation, should comprise Scotland as well as England, for which James I. afterwards hit upon the happy name of Great Britain, leaving to the nineteenth century to give Greater Britain a more fit application to the dependencies and colonies which the natives of the little island have conquered or acquired beyond the Atlantic or in the islands of the Antipodes.

Major dedicated his work in a short preface to his young sovereign James v., whom he describes as celebrated for his noble disposition and high birth, derived from both kingdoms, alluding to his descent as grandson of Henry VII. as well as heir of James IV. The preface is a defence against the charges of a possible critic that he had deviated from the practice of historians in dedicating his history; that a theologian should not venture to write history; and that he has used the style of a theologian rather than an historian. To the first he answers that he has read no dedication by Sallust or Livy, either because they wrote none, or because their dedications are lost. Sallust, indeed, had no reason for a dedication, as he wrote before the Romans had kings (emperors). Livy, perhaps, had no wish to dedicate, deeming it more glorious to offer the fruits of his labours to the Gods and posterity rather than to any mortal. But nearly all the poets, even when they wrote history, dedicated their works. Valerius Maximus invoked Caesar when about to describe the annals not only of his own but of other nations. St. Jerome, St. Augustine, our own Venerable Bede, as well as other ecclesiastical writers, used dedications. He has followed their example, but, to avoid suspicion of flattery, has left the history of recent times to others. The charge that a theologian should not write history he denies. It is the province of a theologian to define matters

Major's dedication to James V.

of faith, religion, and morals, so he cannot be deemed to depart from it when he not only states acts and their authors, but also determines whether they had been rightly or wrongly done. Besides, it would be his aim that the reader of his History should learn not only what had been done, but also how men ought to act, from the experience of so many centuries. For his style, it might have been more polished, but he doubted if more suitable to his subject. If the names of Scottish places and persons were expressed in Latin words the natives would scarcely recognise them. We see from this curious observation how narrowly Major missed writing in the vernacular. Perhaps, could he have printed his book at home, he might have done so. But, no doubt, he also desired to be read by the learned throughout Europe.

It has always been the aim of our kings, he concludes, to act greatly rather than speak elegantly, so it should be the aim of all students to think rightly and understand the matter in hand sharply rather than to write elegantly or rhetorically. Of this the two Scots, John Scotus Erigena[1] and Duns Scotus, Bede, Alcuin, and many others are examples. It is his hope that the king may read happily the history of his race dedicated to his felicity and live to the age of Nestor.

Scheme of the History.

The history which follows narrates in six books in a succinct style the annals of England and Scotland from the earliest times to the marriages of Henry VII.'s daughters, Margaret to James IV. of Scotland, and Mary to Louis XII. of France, and after his death to the Duke of Suffolk. The part relating to Scotland is naturally fuller, but the combination of the two histories was done of set purpose to aid the view which Major insists on that the two crowns should be united by marriage. With the same object, Major treats the English more favourably

---

[1] Although the epithet 'Erigena' is now admitted to be of later date, the current and better opinion seems to be that John Scotus was an Irishman, but Duns Scotus was almost certainly, as Major thought, a Scotchman.—R. Lane Poole, *History of Mediæval Thought,* p. 55 *n* 2.

than our earlier historians. He is the first Scottish advocate for the Union. 'I state this proposition,' he says: 'The Scots ought to prefer no king to the English in the marriage of a female heir, and I am of the same opinion as to the English in a similar case. By this way only two hostile kingdoms flourishing in the same island, of which neither can subdue the other, would be united under one king, and if it is said the Scots would lose their name and kingdom, so would the English, for the king of both would be called king of Britain. Nor would the Scots have any reason to fear the taxes of an English king. I venture to answer for the English king that he would allow them their liberties as the king of Castile allows the people of Aragon. Besides, in case it is for the well-being of the republic, it is proper that taxes should be paid to the king according to the necessity of the occasion. The Scottish nobles, as I think, are unwilling to have one king with power over the whole island, and the English nobles are of like mind, because the nobility would not dare to go against such a king. Yet a single monarch would be useful even to the nobles. They would flourish by justice; no one would dare use force against another. Their homes and families would be more permanent. No foreign king would invade their country, and if they were injured, they would be able without fear to attack others.' *Major an advocate for the Union.* *The nobility wrong in opposing the Union.*

Such opinions were in advance of his age. It is singular how a Scotsman bred in France should have adopted them. Experience must have convinced him that the prosperity of his country pointed to an English union rather than to a French alliance.

Another point on which the opinions of Major are unexpectedly liberal, at least to those who have not followed with minute attention the course of medieval thought, is as to the relation between Church and State. In this connection he repeats the sentiments to which he had given utterance in *Major on Church and State.*

commenting on the Gospel of Matthew, and which he may have learned from the writings of Ockham, D'Ailly, and Gerson. Referring to the excommunication of Alexander II. of Scotland by the Papal Legate on the ground that Alexander had sided with the English barons against King John, he says: 'Perhaps fearing more than was reasonable ecclesiastical censures, he restored Carlisle to the English king. If he had a just title to Carlisle, he had no reason to fear the papal excommunication. Various of his predecessors had held it, nor do I see how he had lost the right, and whatever might be the fact as to that, he could have appealed from the legate to his superior. But perhaps you will object that even the unjust sentence of a pastor (*i.e.* an ecclesiastic in charge of a flock and with power to excommunicate) is to be feared. To which we will easily answer. If it is unjust, it is as if null, and there is no reason to fear it. For an unjust excommunication is no more an excommunication than a dead man is a man. Not only in Britain, but in many other places, men too lightly entangle themselves with ecclesiastical censures. No one, unless he commits mortal sin, ought to be excommunicated either by law or man, and for contumacy alone excommunication is to be pronounced by man. If he will not hear the church, saith the Scripture (*veritas*), let him be as a heathen and publican. Therefore by the opposite argument, if he will hear the church, why should he be ejected from the company of believers? It follows that we think many persons excommunicated are in grace.' This is bold language for an ecclesiastic of the Roman Church, but by allowing excommunication for contumacy, Major leaves a loophole through which his conscience crept when he approved the burning of Patrick Hamilton. This explains too how he and men of like views [1]

---

[1] Jourdain has an interesting and instructive Essay on this subject, dealing with writers of an earlier date (*Excursions Historiques*, 1888, p. 524): 'Mémoire sur La Royauté Française et le Droit Populaire d'après les Ecrivains du Moyen Age'.

were tolerated by the Roman Church, which has always *School opinions as to Church and State.*
allowed considerable latitude to men of learning and ability
who have conceded to the Church the final sentence—the last
word, whether of temporal or eternal condemnation.

When he deals with John's abdication and payment of the
ransom for his crown to the Pope, Major raises the difficulty
whether a king can give the right of his kingdom or fixed pay-
ments out of it to any other person. If he gave the right of
the kingdom to the Turk or any other not the true heir, the
gift would be plainly null. The proof is: 'The king has the
right of the kingdom from a free people, nor can he grant that
right to any one contrary to the will of the people'.

A king cannot be said to act rightly who, without the
counsel of his nobles, declares that his revenues are to be
given away to any one. The proof is: 'Such a tax, without
express or tacit consent, burdens the people, and such a tax the
people are not bound to pay. Further, the contest between
the king and the Church of England was as to goods taken
from that particular church, and specially from the Cistercians.
It is clear, restitution ought to have been made to the particular church. It was idle in John to suppose that because
he gave a quota to Rome, he was absolved from restitution to
the Church from which he had taken the property.' Here the
doctrine of restitution, a favourite and sound doctrine of the
manuals of the Confessional, is very skilfully turned against both
John and the Pope. It is, after all, robbing Paul although you
pay Peter[1]. He concludes with allowing that if John and the
English people agreed to give an annual payment to the Pope
it would be otherwise, for it does not concern the king's purse,
but is given by the people itself. These are almost the constitutional principles embodied by the barons in the charters
of the Liberties of England, but which Buchanan generally

---

[1] The proverb is more often cited in the reverse form, but is known in both forms.

Constitutional Doctrines.

gets the credit of introducing into Scotland. He may have derived them in part at least from his old master. When we read Barbour's *Bruce* or Blind Harry's *Wallace*, we trace their parentage to a still earlier date. They were the fruit of the War of Independence. Perhaps they may be traced to a more distant epoch, to the resistance which Galgacus and our remote Celtic forefathers made to the Roman legions. Major tells an anecdote which shows they existed before the War of Independence in the breast of the patriot leader. Wallace, he says, always had in his mouth lines his tutor had taught him :—

> ' Dico tibi verum, Libertas optima rerum ;
> Nunquam servili sub nexu vivite, fili.'

With equal distinctness Major, in treating of the succession of Bruce, states he does not place Bruce's right on the ground of priority of descent, but because Baliol, by surrendering the crown to Edward, forfeited his right. 'A free people gives the strength to the first king whose power depends on the whole people. Fergus the first had no other right. I say the same of the kings of Judea ordained by God.' He further argues that the people can depose for his demerits a king and his successors, founding on the precedents of the Roman kingship which was abolished, and the Carlovingian dynasty which was founded when Pepin by the will of the people deposed the Merovingian line.

Government founded on the will of the people.

The proof from the establishment of the Roman republic shows another source from which views in favour of the foundation of government on the will of the people were drawn by scholars in the time of Major. The Greek and Roman classics, above all Livy, recently translated into French, and soon after into Scotch by Bellenden, presented the noble spectacle of a free republic. It is noticeable that Major frequently reflects on the tyranny and want of patriotism of the nobles. Wallace is his hero rather than Bruce, and in a fine passage which reminds us of the poem of Dante in the

Convito[1], he argues that 'there is no true nobility but virtue and its acts. Vulgar nobility is nothing but a windy mode of talk.' He laughs at his countrymen, who think themselves all cousins of the king, and says he used to argue with them jocularly in this way : 'They would grant no one was noble unless both his parents were noble. If so, was Adam noble or not? If he was not, they denied the premiss. If he was, then so were all his children. So it follows either that all men are noble or none.' It is evident that we are listening to a representative of the Commons, to a forerunner of Robert Burns in the strangely different garb of a medieval philosopher. A similar or cognate argument was expressed in the popular rhyme of the English peasants—

> 'When Adam delved, and Eve span,
> Who was then the gentleman?'

Like all clear-sighted men at this period, Major saw the urgency of reform in the Church. He approves the saying of James I., that David I. had injured the Crown by lavish grants to Bishops and Monks. He expresses his regret at the poverty of parishes and parish churches in Scotland in comparison with England, at the gross abuses of pluralities and non-residence, and his surprise that the Scottish prelates had not earlier applied some part of their great revenues to founding Universities. He especially condemns the wealthy abbots who live in the court more than in the cloister, who think they do well when they enrich their convent by oppressing the poor labourers of the ground. The true end of religion is to subdue the lusts of the flesh, and wealth is adverse to this end. When

Abuses in the Church condemned.

---

[1] ' It follows then from this,
That all are high or base,
Or that in time there never was
Beginning to our race.

. . . .

Where virtue is there is
A nobleman, although
Not where there is a nobleman
Must virtue be also.'
The Convito, Fourth Book (Miss E. Price Sayers' translation).

he describes Bishop Kennedy's character he blames him for holding the Priory of Pittenweem *in commendam* along with so great a See as St. Andrews, and for the cost of his sumptuous tomb; and he raises the question whether a bishop has more than a qualified right of property in the revenue he derives from the church. In the passages of his History in which he attacks the oppression of the nobles and the corruption of the ecclesiastical dignitaries we recall the language of the Satires of Henryson, Dunbar, and Lindsay [1]. Against the abuses of ill-regulated monasteries Major more than once inveighs [2], and though he maintains the binding nature of vows, he admits the difficulty of the question. On the critical point of the privilege of ecclesiastics to be exempt from the judgment of lay courts, while he takes, as might be expected, the side of the Church in discussing the struggle between Henry II. and Becket, he allows this was not by divine right, and might be otherwise in special circumstances. He even goes so far as to condemn the multiplication of miracles, and remarks (though earlier as well as later examples of the same train of reasoning may be found) that miracles do not prove holiness, for John the Baptist, the holiest child born of woman, wrought none, and that a vow of chastity might be a vow of the foolish virgins if it hurt the state.

With regard to the facts of his History Major shows a wonderfully sound historical instinct, distinguishing truth from the fables with which the Scottish annals were then encrusted. His work is a sketch, and much is omitted; but the student who reads it will have little to unlearn. In this respect he is far superior to his contemporary Boece, and even to Buchanan, who copied Boece in the earlier part of Scottish history.

---

[1] With these passages in the History may be compared his denunciation in his Commentary on St. Matthew of 'the grasping abbots who make things hard for the husbandmen', fol. lxxiv. verso 2.

[2] Compare Commentary on St. Matthew, fol. lxxiii. verso 2: 'If I were as rich as Midas, I would rather throw my money into the Seine than found a religious house where men and women take their meals together.'

He discards at once the foundation fable of the Scottish kings being descended from Scota the daughter of Pharaoh, and takes the firm ground of Bede as to their Irish origin, and inclines to the further opinion, which may be true though not proved, that they came from Spain to Ireland. The Picts, following Bede and their own traditions, he states, came also by way of Ireland from Scythia, and he ascribes probably rightly their name to the practice of painting their bodies. Although he did not succeed in detecting the insertion of forty kings between Fergus I. Mac Fercha and Fergus II. Mac Erc, he shows his distrust of it by reckoning only fifteen where Fordun and Wyntoun had made forty. Buchanan, who ought to have known better, has compiled a list still longer and less intelligible, which corrupted Scottish History at the fountainhead till the sources were purified first by Father Innes, and more completely in our day by Mr. Skene. It is significant of how far Major was in advance not merely of his own but of a later age that Dr. Mackenzie, writing in 1708 his memoir of Major, supposes the reduction of the number of the kings to be a misprint. *Major's criticism of early Scottish History.*

He argues from the life of Ninian as well as Bede that the Picts and Britons had occupied Scotland before the Scots migrated from Ireland. Bede's authority and his own knowledge as a Lothian man of the dedication of the Church at Whittingham to St. Oswald, enable him to assert the fact of the whole of Lothian having been in the time of Bede under the Northumbrian kings. He refers to the Commentaries of Bede and to Alcuin as proof of the learning of the Northumbrian ecclesiastics of the eighth century, though he says they were not well versed in the knotty questions of the Schoolmen and the Sorbonne. He says boldly that the Church of St. Columba had priests and monks but not bishops, in which he is in substance right, even though it be held proved that there was an order of bishops whose only known function of preeminence was the ordination of priests. For how different was such a bishop from the lordly diocesan prelates of Major's own time! He gives correctly the date of the union of the Picts and Scots in the middle of the ninth century under Kenneth Macalpine, and leaves as a doubtful point what is still doubtful—how long Abernethy had been the chief seat of the Pictish Church before its transfer to St. Andrews. He remarks that the Picts held St. Andrew in great honour, from which he jumps to the possibly sound conclusion that the Picts held the richer and level parts of the country, while the Scots occupied the mountains. The Anglo-Saxon period of English history and the contemporary history of Scotland from Kenneth Macalpine to Malcolm Canmore is very rapidly sketched, and there are many errors in the attempt to synchronise the kings.

Independent view of the later history.
After Canmore the history is more clear and accurate, and though the reigns of the English kings are slurred, a distinct portrait of each of the Scottish monarchs is presented: Alexander the Bold ('audax'), who imitated his father in bravery and zeal for justice; the good king David; Malcolm, who followed the piety of his ancestors; the long reign of William the Lion; Alexander the Second, who fought with John on the side of the English barons, and lost nothing his ancestors had gained, observing justice during his whole life; the third Alexander, who rivalled his father in the goodness of his reign. The War of Independence is told as might be expected by a Scottish patriot, and the true characters of Wallace and Bruce are defended against the attacks of Caxton's Chronicle; but he rejects as fabulous the visit of Wallace to France, which subsequent research has confirmed, on the ground that this visit is not mentioned by the French or the Latin Chronicles of Scotland. David II. he characterises, though brave, as a weak king, and he blames the want of patriotism which led him to name an English prince as his successor. The second and third Robert are less distinctly drawn. James I.

is the finest portrait. It has been copied in all subsequent histories. 'In person short, but stout and robust, of the finest intellect but somewhat passionate. Skilled in games, he threw the stone and hammer further than any one, and was a swift runner. He was a trained musician, and second to none in the modulation of his voice. In harp playing he surpassed, like another Orpheus, the Irish and Highland Scots, the masters of that instrument. All these arts he learned in France and England during his long captivity. In Scottish poetry he was very skilful, and very many of his works and songs are still held by the Scotch in memory as the best of their kind. ... He was not inferior to, perhaps was greater than, Thomas Randolph in administering justice. He excelled his father, grandfather, and great-grandfather in virtue, nor do I prefer,' he concludes, 'any of the Stewarts and their predecessors, without counting the present boy (James v.), to James I.' *Characters of the Jameses.*

Of James II. he says, many gave him the palm amongst active kings because he applied all his zeal to war and showed himself equal to any knight. 'I place,' however, 'his father before him both in intellect and courage, but in temper he much resembled his father.' Of James III. he speaks with less praise, giving only the negative encomium, of which his countrymen are fond, that there have been many worse kings both abroad and at home. James IV. was not inferior to James II., as appears from his deeds. 'Many of the Scots,' he remarks, 'secretly compare the Stewarts to the horses of Mar, which are good in youth but bad in old age; but I do not share this view. The Stewarts have preserved the Scots in good peace, and have held in hand the kingdom left by the Bruces undiminished.' There is a boldness in judging and distributing praise and blame to the kings very characteristic of Major and his countrymen. His judgment is not that of a partisan, but of a contemplative historian. Not less interesting, pointed, clear, and fair are the brief remarks which he makes on the character of his countrymen than on those of the kings. His foreign residence helped him to gauge their insular vanity and intense family pride. But it had not diminished his patriotism. Love of his country and desire for its true welfare is everywhere conspicuous in his writings. 'Our native soil attracts us with a secret and inexpressible sweetness and does not permit us to forget it', he wrote to Alexander Stewart, the archbishop of St. Andrews, while he was still living in Paris, in the dedication of the edition of his Commentary on the Fourth Book of the Sentences [1].

It was during Major's second residence in Paris that Francis I.—who, like James V., had at first hesitated to prosecute the Reformers, and even leant towards them, partly from policy, as a means of attacking the Emperor through the German Lutherans, and partly from scholarly tastes, which made him a patron of the Renaissance—went over to the side of the Old Church. He had tried to persuade Erasmus to return to France and preside over the new Royal College, in which the three ancient classical languages, Hebrew, Greek, and Latin, were to be taught; but Erasmus was too prudent. Francis had twice saved from the stake Berquin, the translator of Erasmus, a man, like Hamilton, of good family, but on a third declaration of heretical opinions abandoned him to his fate.

The Sorbonne condemns Erasmus.

The Doctors of the Sorbonne were bitter enemies of Erasmus, and, led by Major's old patron, Noel Beda, now their Syndic, they induced the University to condemn his principal works. His 'Colloquies' had been so popular, that a Paris printer issued 24,000 copies of one edition; they were even used as a text-book in some of the University classes. The Theological Faculty had already taken the alarm in 1526, and petitioned Parliament to suppress the work, but nothing was done. Two years later Beda, in the name of the Theological Faculty, applied to the University. The Faculties of Canon Law and

---

[1] Appendix II., p. 420.

Medicine, and the French Nation, sided with the Faculty of Theology in condemnation of a book dangerous to youth. The German Nation was willing to interdict its use in the classes. The Nations of Picardy and Normandy desired to write to the author, asking him to correct his errors. The Rector embraced the more severe view, which had the balance of authority in its favour, and the book was absolutely condemned.

Beda was at this time so powerful in the University, and even with the mob of Paris, aptly styled by Michelet the false democracy, that he was called the King of Paris. The influence of his mother Ann, a fervent Catholic, drew Francis in the direction of Rome. The excess of Lutheranism began to show itself in the Anabaptists. The monarchs of Europe began to fear that their authority might be impugned as well as that of the Pope. A comparatively trifling incident is said to have finally decided Francis. Some one—no one knew who—broke an image of the Virgin and Child on the Sunday before Easter 1525, in the Rue des Rosiers in Paris. It was at once attributed to the Reformers. *Changes in Francis I.'s attitude.*

The University, led by Beda, went in solemn procession, preceded by 500 youths with candles, to the place of the sacrilege, deposited their candles, and returned for a solemn expiatory service at the Church of St. Catherine. Two days later the King headed a still larger procession, in which the Princes of the Blood Royal, the Ambassadors, the High Officials of the Court, the Church, and the University, took part, and replaced the broken image with one in silver, amidst the acclamations of the people.

A condemnation of the translation of the New Testament, prepared by the Faculty of Theology in 1527, was at last issued in 1531. Encouraged by this success, and the martyrdom of several less conspicuous Lutherans which followed that of Berquin in 1529, Beda ventured on the condemnation of

Le Miroir de l'âme pécheresse, a mystical and devotional work by the king's sister Margaret, Queen of Navarre, and he attacked the Royal Professors, who were now beginning to carry out a pet project of Francis—the institution of the new College for free instruction in Latin, Greek, and Hebrew. His zeal had carried him a step too far. For these offences he was compelled to make a public apology, was imprisoned during the King's pleasure, and the uncrowned king, one of the many victims to the 'vaulting ambition which o'erleaps itself', died a captive at Mont St. Michel. Francis I., like Henry VIII., was not a religious but a despotic monarch, who would brook no rival in Church or State.

The Sorbonne and Henry VIII.'s Divorce. It is not certain whether Major joined the Doctors of the Sorbonne in their sanction given in January 1530 to the divorce of Henry VIII., contrary to the wishes of the fanatical but orthodox Beda. The records of the period have been destroyed; but as the opinion was issued during his residence, it is probable he concurred in it. While we condemn this act, it must be remembered that it was in one aspect a declaration of the independence of the temporal power against the Pope, which would find favour with the Gallican Doctors. Francis I., in an angry letter to the Parliament of Paris, expressly condemned Beda's proposal to refer the matter to the Pope, as trenching on 'the liberties of the Gallican Church and the independence of the Theological Council, for there is no privilege belonging to the realm on which we are more firmly determined to insist'.

Loyola, Calvin, Rabelais. Michelet notes that during these years three men, different in every respect except in the greatness of their fame, came to Paris to complete their education—Ignatius Loyola, who commenced his education in grammar at Montaigu in 1528, John Calvin, who entered the College of Ste. Barbe in 1523, and Francis Rabelais. Rabelais's college has not been discovered, but probably he was in Paris from 1524 to 1530. With none of them can Major have had much sympathy; but it marks the pregnant character of the time and place that they produced such contrasts as the ascetic militant founder of the Society of Jesus, whose rule was to surpass even Papal absolutism; the Protestant theologian whose discipline, almost as strict as that of the Jesuits, and founded on principles as plausible, once its premisses are admitted, was to succeed the Lutheran as the latest form of the reformed Church; and the satirist whose coarse and giant laughter, a revulsion from the rules alike of the old orders and of the new sects, was to shake the foundations of the Church in France and become the parent of the best and worst in modern French literature. The irony of Erasmus, and the satire of Rabelais, were almost the only weapons which could be used by reformers who wished to escape the fate of Berquin. Major himself came in for a chance stroke of the lash of Rabelais, who places amongst the books in the library of St. Victor, 'Majoris de Modo faciendi boudinos'—'Major on the Art of making Puddings.'

Before finally leaving Paris for Scotland Major completed his labours in Logic by issuing a new edition of the Introduction to Aristotle's Logic in 1527, and a new treatise, Quaestiones Logicales, in 1528, and his labours in Philosophy by an edition of the Ethics of Aristotle in 1530, and his labours in Theology by new editions of his Commentaries on the First, Second, and Third Books of the Sentences in 1528-1530. But the chief employment of this portion of his life was an elaborate Commentary and Harmony of the Four Gospels, which he had projected in 1518, when he published his Exposition of St. Matthew, and now in 1529 published as a complete work. Each Gospel has a separate dedicatory letter. St. Matthew is dedicated to his chief Scottish patron, James Beaton, Archbishop of St. Andrews; St. Mark to his old college friend, John Bouillache, Curate of St. James in Paris; St. Luke to James Dunbar, Archbishop of Glasgow; and St. John to his

Major's final published works.

His Biblical Commentaries.

old pupil, Robert Senalis, now Bishop of Vence. The Doubts and Difficulties he had inserted in the earlier edition of the Commentary on St. Matthew were not reprinted, but the complete work had an appendix of four questions:— (1) Whether the Law of Grace is the only true Law; (2) What are the degrees of Catholic Truth; (3) On the number of the Evangelists; (4) On the site of the Promised Land.

Dedication to James Beaton.

The letter to Beaton explains the object which Major had in view in this work. It was to show the Harmony of the Gospels with each other and of each in itself, and to preserve the tradition of the doctrine of the Roman Church. In carrying out this intention he has refuted the errors of Theophylact [1], the Bulgarian Bishop, and of the Wycliffite, Hussite, and Lutheran sects. The errors of others he has noted without naming them, 'for Christians have been taught not to call a brother Racha.'

· He has dedicated it to James Beaton, because he owed to him a good part of his studies, alluding doubtless to the offices he had held at Glasgow and St. Andrews, and who became a teacher on this subject, was suitable to Beaton's name, profession, race, education, and conduct (*mores*). 'His name "Jacob" means a supplanter, as he had been of heresy, and "Beaton" signifies a noble herb, an antidote to poison, as he had shown himself of the vigorous poison of the Lutherans. His profession and office made it his duty to study and preach the Gospels, and his race, as that of every illustrious family, to protect the Church. Finally, his conduct in removing, not without the envy of many, a noble but unhappy follower of the Lutheran heresy.' The work which follows

His orthodoxy united with a reforming spirit.

answers to the design. It is a rigidly orthodox commentary, in which Major allows himself much less freedom than in his

---

[1] Theophylact, Archbishop of Bulgaria (d. 1112) achieved a lasting reputation by his Commentaries on the Gospels, the Acts the Epistles of St. Paul, and the minor Prophets.—Hardwicke's *Church History of the Middle Ages*, p. 273.

writings on the Books of the Sentences, or in his History, or even in the Doubts which he had inserted in the earlier edition of the Commentary on St. Matthew. If he spares others who have held erroneous views, he never hesitates to condemn in the strongest language the heretics who had denied the doctrine of transubstantiation,—Berengarius, who had been condemned by the Council of Vercellae, Wyclif by that of Constance, and the Germans of his own time who had revived the same heresy, and of whom he did not know whether Oecolampadius, Zwingle, or Luther was the worst. Transubstantiation, he vehemently reiterates, is the doctrine of Scripture, of the Church, and of the Fathers of the Church. It is also the doctrine 'of our Theological Faculty of Paris[1]. Whoever denies it is a foolish heretic.' He defends the monastic life and the celibacy of the clergy against the Lutherans[2], but admits that there were monasteries and nunneries which required reform, and again, as in his History, he mentions with approval the case of the English nunnery which, when he was pursuing his studies at Cambridge, he had seen transformed into a college by the Bishop of Ely[3]. So too he strongly condemns the bestowal of livings on unworthy priests, or even the preference of a less worthy candidate and the pluralities which were so common in the Church in his day. 'Those deceive themselves,' he says, 'who think that the approval even of the Supreme Pontiff can reconcile such things to the dictates of Conscience[4].' He insists on the duty of preaching, especially by the prelates of the Church. In a curious passage[5] which seems to have a personal reference, in commenting on the fact that some of Christ's kinsmen did not acknowledge Him, he adds 'just as our relations treat us as mad because we spend

---

[1] In Joann. caput vi., fol. cclxxxviii.   [2] In Matth. fol. lxxii.
[3] John Alcock, Bishop of Ely, was the Reformer of the Nunnery of St. Radegunde, which he converted into Jesus College, Cambridge.—Mullinger, p. 321.
[4] In Matth. fol. lxxx.   [5] In Marc. fol. cxvi.

our whole activity in philosophy and theology. They wish us rather to apply ourselves to the law to gain honour and wealth, and take offence at all knowledge which is not lucrative. According to their false estimation we exist for them and not for our own salvation and the glory of God. For they say, What profit does he bring to us? Let his library, with its books, be burnt. And they think the more sublimely any one philosophises, and thereby magnifies the power of God, that he is so much the greater fool[1].'

Such have been the recriminations of those who pursue knowledge for its own sake, and of those who follow it for gain, in all ages; but probably at no time was the contrast sharper than between the monastic student of the middle ages, who had taken the vow of poverty, and the practical man his relative or neighbour, who devoted his life to the acquisition of wealth. While strenuously maintaining the worship of the Saints against the Lutherans and other heretics, he admits that there was a possibility of abuse which must be corrected by the proper ecclesiastical authorities[2]. The use of Images in Churches he altogether approves, and condemns the revival by Wyclif and Luther of the heresy of the Greek Church in the time of Leo the Iconoclast with regard to them[3]. These examples may suffice to indicate the spirit of the teaching of Major as a biblical Commentator. He stands firm in the old paths of the Roman and Catholic Church, and treats all deviations from its doctrine as pestilent and poisonous heresy. But like the best Romanists of his age, he favours reforms within the Church and by the Church itself.

The last of Major's published works was a return to his earliest master. The Ethics of Aristotle, with Commentaries by himself, were printed at the press of Badius Ascensius in 1530,[4] shortly before his return to Scotland.

---

[1] In Marc. fol. cxvii.
[3] In Joann. fol. cccxiii.
[2] In Joann. fol. cccxxii.
[4] Appendix I., p. 407.

More interesting even than the subject of the work is the Preface which preserves the memory of the relations between Major and the great minister of Henry VIII. As it contains several references to his own life, and is one of the best of his numerous dedications, we give a translation of what were probably his last published words, for the twenty years he still survived were spent in other pursuits than authorship[1]. *(Dedication of Major's Commentary on the Ethics of Aristotle to Wolsey.)*

On the Kalends of June 1530 he wrote to Wolsey the following dedicatory letter:—

' To the most Reverend Father and Lord in Christ, Lord Thomas Wolsey, Cardinal Presbyter of the Holy Roman Church by the title of St. Cecilia, Archbishop of York, Primate of England, and Legate *a Latere* of the Apostolic See, John Major of Haddington, with all observance, greeting.

' I have often and long determined with myself, and conceived in my mind, most bountiful of Prelates, to dedicate to some English prince the first fruits of my poor thoughts, such as they are, and that for good reasons as I think. The first of them, not to be diffuse, is the love of our common country, which is innate in all living creatures; for we, separated only by a small space, are enclosed together in one Britain, the most celebrated island in all Europe, as in a ship upon a great ocean. My second reason is our community of religion and of studies. My third and, not to multiply words, my last and strongest reason is the desire to avoid ingratitude, the least note of which was deemed even by the Persians the most odious stain. For I have been received and honoured by Englishmen with such frequent hospitality, such humane and genial converse, such friendly intercourse, that I cannot be longer silent without showing a forgetful mind. Forty[2] years ago, if I reckon rightly, when I first left my father's house and went through England to Paris, I was received and retained with so great courtesy by the English, that during a whole year I learned the first rudiments of a good education in arts in the very celebrated College of Cambridge, now illustrious by the name of Christ. Afterwards, so far as I was permitted by the never-changing

---
[1] For the original, see Appendix II., p. 448.
[2] It was really thirty-six or thirty-seven, for Major went to Paris in 1493, after, as this Preface informs us, a year's residence in England.

sea (*per mare perpetuum*), I always made my journeys to and from France through England. Besides, what I hold and will always hold in fresh and constant memory so long as there is breath in my body, it is now the fourth year since your Grace, Most Reverend Legate, most bountiful and chief of the ecclesiastical dignitaries of England, entertained with the old hospitality of Christians one of my humble condition when I was again making my journey to France, and invited me to the College of Letters, then recently founded by your magnificent beneficence at Oxford[1], to do the best I could to enlighten it by my presence and teaching, and made me the offer of most splendid remuneration. But so great a love possessed me for the University of Paris, my mother, and for my fellows in study, besides the desire to complete the books which I had already begun, that I could not accept the post so freely offered and so honourable. Now therefore, that I may not seem altogether forgetful of such great benefits, and that I may produce what during so many years I have laboured with, I inscribe and dedicate to you, who are both so great a Prince in ecclesiastical rank and the Maecenas not only of all theologians but of all men of letters, that most celebrated work on Ethics, written by Aristotle, the Prince of philosophers in the judgment of many, and explained by my own commentaries, of however little value these may be. As in the rest of his writings he has surpassed others, in this work he seems to have surpassed himself, that is the power of human nature. For in almost all his opinions he agrees with the Catholic and truest Christian faith in all its integrity. He constantly asserts the Free Will of man. He declares with gravity that suicide, to avoid the sad things of life, is the mark not of a truly brave but of a timid spirit. He separates honest pleasures which good men may seek after from the foul allurements the Turks propose for themselves. He places the happiness which man may attain to in the exercise of the heroic virtues. And he pursues with admirable judgment the examination of the two kinds of life, I mean the active and the contemplative, which were figured in the Old Testament by the sisters Rachel and Leah, and to us by Martha and Magdalene[2].

---

[1] Christ Church was begun by Wolsey in 1525, but never completed on his plan. The Cardinal's College, as it came to be called, was forfeited by Henry VIII., and finished on an inferior scale by the king.—Brewer's *Henry* VIII.

[2] Mary, the sister of Martha, supposed by mediæval commentators to be Mary Magdalene.

For he applies the one to the life of the gods, the other to the life of mortals.

In fine, in so great and manifold a work, if it be read as we explain it, you meet scarcely a single opinion unworthy of a Christian man. Wherefore, Most Magnificent Father, as you lately received me with such humanity and benevolence, we beg you now to accept this new birth, which, even if it were, as I wish, much better than it is, was long ago your due, and is now at last dedicated from my heart to your Eminence.'

Do the Latin superlatives and high-flown style strike us as antiquated and exaggerated? Let us recognise qualities which are better than any style, however perfect in taste and proportion—the ardent patriotism, the Academic spirit, the recognition of the nobility of the morals of the heathen philosopher, and the warm gratitude for Wolsey's kind offices. Let us remember too that when Wolsey had offered to place Major in the College which he was endowing with more than royal munificence, he was at the summit of his power; but when this dedication was written he had fallen so low that in England there was scarcely any one 'so poor to do him reverence.' In October of the previous year he had been prosecuted under the Statute of Provisors for accepting the Legatine office, which entailed the penalties of Praemunire and placed all he possessed at the king's mercy. On the 17th of that month he had been compelled to surrender the Great Seal; an inventory of all his goods had been taken, and two days later he had confessed the charge and submitted himself to the king's pleasure. Though pardoned in February 1530, and restored to the Archbishopric, he had been finally deprived of his other great benefices, Winchester and St. Albans. He had retired to his diocese in failing health and fallen spirits, and at the time when Major was writing this dedication he was travelling by slow stages from Grantham to Newark, and from Newark to Southwell, where he spent Whitsuntide.[1]

Time and tone of Preface honourable to Major.

---

[1] Brewer's *Reign of Henry* VIII., ii. 413.

He lived till 29th November 1530, and wrote many piteous and unavailing letters to the king to be restored to some portion of the property of which he had been stripped, and, above all, that the Colleges of Ipswich and Christ Church might be spared. They were the darling objects of his beneficence, and intended to perpetuate his name. 'By Wolsey himself,' writes Mr. Brewer, 'the loss of power, the forfeiture of his estate, and even his exile to York were regarded with indifference compared with the ruin of his colleges. For recovery of the former he made little or no effort. For the preservation of his colleges he bestirred himself with ceaseless and untiring energy, employing all the little influence he possessed, or believed he possessed, with men in power to rescue them from the hands of the spoiler.'

It may also be noted to the credit both of Wolsey and Major that Wolsey was a pronounced Thomist, and had even acquired the epithet of *Thomisticus*. Yet this had not hindered the Cardinal from offering the post of teacher in his college to one who like Major inclined to the position of the Scotist philosophy, and did not prevent Major, while insisting on the Freedom of the Will, the key-note of Duns Scotus' separation from the doctrine of Aquinas, from expressing his gratitude and dedicating his work to Wolsey.

To both the great Minister and the great Schoolman the Renaissance had imparted some of its reconciling influences. When we consider Major's work as a whole we are sensible that he was more in place in the Sorbonne than he would have been at Christ Church, in a college which retained the old subjects and methods of teaching rather than in one which aimed at adopting the new learning. Still his connection with the college ennobled by the name of Christ at Cambridge, when a student, and his narrow escape from becoming a Professor in the college which received the same name at Oxford, and favoured a reform in education, was something more than an accident in his life. It shows how near he stood, and was deemed by some of his contemporaries to stand, to the parting of the ways between the Mediæval and the Modern plans of University education. But when he was summoned to his own country as a director of public instruction, it was the Mediæval Scholasticism and not the Modern Humanism that he followed both at Glasgow and St. Andrews. He was a Modern only in Logic, and in the restricted and technical sense in which that word was used to denote the school which made the doctrine of 'Terms' the cardinal part of Logic. He was a keen reformer of ecclesiastical abuses, but was not prepared for reform either in dogmatic theology[1] or educational methods.

The Bibliography of Major's works compiled by the learned zeal of Mr. T. Graves Law, Librarian of the Library of the Writers to the Signet, and the kind aid of the keepers of the principal Libraries where his works are still to be found, is a valuable key to the biography of Major, and an interesting chapter in the history of the early French press. For it was in France that all his works were printed. The art of printing, like the other fine arts which were the offspring of the Revival of Letters, was a late comer to Northern Britain. Chepman and Millar's press, in the Southgait of Edinburgh, issued its first sheets, the *primitiae* of Scottish printing, in 1508, and its last, so far as is known, in June 1510. A single sheet of eight small leaves which contains the *Compassio beatae Mariae* is the solitary record of the names of John Story the printer and Carolus Stute the publisher. A copy of *The Buke of the Howlat*, discovered by Mr. David Laing, in the binding of some early Protocol Books, completes the brief sum of Scottish printing between 1510 and 1520, one of the most active periods of the early press of France and Germany. The first work of Thomas Davidson, the next Scottish printer, did not appear till 1542, when Major had for twelve years

Bibliography of his works illustrates his Biography.

---

[1] This is strikingly shown by his dedication in 1530 of a new edition of his Commentary on the First Book of the *Sentences* to John Mayr (or Major), the Suabian called Eck, from his birthplace, the most celebrated champion of the Church against Luther. Appendix II., p. 449.

ceased publishing. Necessity as well as choice, due to his long residence in France, made him select Lyons and Paris as the birthplace of his literary children. There was no press in his native country which could have issued his voluminous works, and few buyers had there been such a press. How different was the case in France, whose famous printers vied with each other in producing them, and the demand was sufficient to produce editions of the same work by different publishers, and frequent revised editions of some by Major himself. A rapid survey of these will illustrate at once the activity of the French press and the popularity of Major. Major seems to have commenced by printing at Paris in 1503 his first Logical Lectures on *Exponibilia*, at the press of John Lambert, and two years later he issued his Commentaries on the logical *Summulae* of Peter the Spaniard from the press of Francis Fradin in Lyons. In 1508 John De Vingle, another Lyons printer, father of the more famous Peter, the Calvinist printer of Geneva, published his whole lectures on Logic as a Regent in Arts, which were sold in the same town by Stephen Queygnard, and of which there was a new edition in 1516. He had also in 1505 issued, along with Magister Ortiz, in Paris, the *Medulla Dialectices* of Jerome Pardus. In 1508 his Commentary on the Fourth Book of the Sentences was printed by Philip Pigouchet, and sold by Ponset le Preux, and it was republished by Badius Ascensius in 1516; and in 1516 his lectures in Arts were reprinted in Paris by John Grandjon, and sold by Dyonysius Roce.

Why several of these earlier works were published at Lyons has not been clearly ascertained. It may be conjectured that as Lyons was as early as Paris [1] a centre of printing [2], and already possessed forty printers in the fifteenth century, although Paris had more than double that number, some chance introduction may have led Major to resort to them.

---

[1] Monteil: *Histoire des Français*, iii. p. 305.
[2] Brunet, *Supplément par un Bibliophile*, s.v. LYONS, notes that it was then the chief market for books, as Frankfort afterwards, and now Leipzig.

The Lyons printers and publishers employed by Major were Francis Fradin (1505), Stephen Queygnard (1508), John De Vingle (1508), Martin Boillon (1516). An edition of the *Summulae* of Peter the Spaniard was published in Venice by Lazarus de Soardis in 1506, and another at Caen in 1520. With these exceptions, and after 1516, Paris became his sole place of publication, and his principal publishers were John Grandjon and Badius Ascensius. But besides these we find frequently the following Parisian printers and publishers: John Parvus (Petit), who appears to have been a partner of Badius: Constantine Lepus, James le Messier, J. Borlier, John Lambert, Dyonysius Roce, William Anabat, Giles Gourmont, the partner of Petit after the death of Badius, Durand Gerlier, and Johannes Frillon. *His numerous printers and publishers.*

Several of the last-named printers, with the exception of Petit and Gourmont, were probably pirates, who then as now preyed upon the works of celebrated and fashionable authors, and may be left in the obscurity they merit. Grandjon and Badius deserve a brief record. Of Grandjon little is known except that he was one of the most voluminous publishers or bibliopoles of the University of Paris, and that his shop was in the world-famed Clos Bruneau, with whose name the Parisian students startled the ears of the watch by their cry, 'Allez au Clos Bruneau, vous trouverez à qui parler'. His sign, which hung over his shop, and was engraved as a device on his books, was a group of great rushes (magni junci) in a marsh, a pun on his name of Grand or Grant Jon. *John Grandjon.*

Jodocus Badius was a still more celebrated printer, and deserves recognition by Scottish historical students, for to his press we owe the two first printed histories of Scotland, that of Hector Boece, as well as that of John Major. Born at Asc, near Brussels (whence his name Ascensius), about 1462, after finishing his education at Ghent and Brussels, and visiting Italy, he settled in Lyons as a lecturer on Latin, but derived probably a larger income as corrector of the press for *Jodocus Badius.*

Jean Treschel, one of the earliest Lyons printers. Marrying the daughter of Treschel, he migrated to Paris about 1498, and there began to print on his own account. His press, of which a facsimile is given on the title-page of his books, was established in the Aedes Ascensianae, and, till his death about 1536, was the most prolific in Paris. No less than 400 volumes, the greater part folios and quartos, issued from it. They included the most important Latin classics, on several of which he wrote a Commentary, a translation by his own hand of Sebastian Brand's *Ship of Fools*, and many historical, philosophical, and theological works. He was employed not only by French but also by English and Scottish authors, who were doubtless attracted to a printer who was also a scholar. He began to print for Major in 1516, and continued to do so down to 1530. His eldest daughter, the wife of Robert Stephen or Etienne, became the ancestress of a famous race of printers. The second was the wife of Jean Roygny, who carried on his father-in-law's press, and the youngest of Michael Vascosanus, also a well-known Parisian printer. His son Conrad became a Protestant, and retired with his brother-in-law Robert Stephen to Geneva. If the epigram of his grandson Henry Stephen could be trusted, Badius must have had several other children, though his books were his most numerous progeny. A sentence which he inscribed on several of his volumes may be commended to publishers:—' Aere Meret Badius Laudem Auctorum Arte Legentium,' which may be freely translated:—

> 'His authors praised his grateful heart,
> His readers praised his graceful art.'

In one of Major's volumes Badius celebrates the author in Latin verse[1], and Major frequently records his gratitude for

---

[1] IODOCUS BADIUS LECTORI.
Quartum Maioris, Lector studiose, suprema
　Iam tersum lima, perlege, disce, cole.
Quem si cum reliquis trutina perpenderis eque :
　Pridem alijs maior, se modo maior erit. [From the *In Quartum*, ed. 1521.]

LIFE OF JOHN MAJOR

the care of the press of Badius. One of these passages will appeal to the feelings both of the reader and the writer for the press. 'I had no human aid', he writes, 'except that of the printer, who has laboured with the greatest vigilance that commas, periods, and other stops should not be left out, although the copy was written by various hands; for my amanuensis was sometimes prevented by the lectures which he had to attend, and my own handwriting was difficult for others to read'.[1]

Another point of contact between Major and the early Parisian press deserves mention. Uldericus Guerinck or Ulric Gering, the French Caxton, or first Parisian printer, was closely associated with the College of Montaigu. During his life he was a constant benefactor of its poor students, and by his will he left it the half of his goods and the third of the debts due to him. With the proceeds of this legacy the College bought the farm of Daunet, near the Marne, and the Hotel de Vézelay, which was situated between Montaigu and the College of St. Michel. On the latter site were built rooms for the classes of Grammar and Arts soon after 1510, the year when Gering died, and in the Chapel of the College a portrait of its benefactor was hung with an inscription describing him as 'Proto-Typographus Parisius 1469', and recording his benefaction. In these class-rooms Major may have lectured, and in that chapel he must have frequently worshipped[2].

Ulric Gering, the first Parisian printer, a benefactor of Montaigu.

In 1531 Major returned from Paris to St. Andrews, and resumed his lectures on Theology. Three years after, the death of Hugh Spens[3] caused a vacancy in the office of Provost of St. Salvator, and Major was appointed. The first entry of his name in that office after his return is on 4th November 1535, when he was again elected an Assessor of the Dean of Faculty of Arts. He was annually re-elected, at least till 1538. He was

Major at St. Andrews. Provost of St. Salvator.

---

[1] Exordium Libri Quarti Sententiarum. Appendix II., p. 439.
[2] *Annals of Parisian Typography*, by Rev. W. Parr Gresswell, 1815, the frontispiece of which is the portrait of Gering.
[3] His tomb bears the inscription, 'Obiit anno domini 1534, et 21 die Julii.'

also one of the Rector's Assessors from 1532 to 1544, with which was generally joined the office of Rector's Deputy: the Assessor was one of the Council of the Rector, and the Deputy his representative when absent. In 1539 he founded, along with William Manderston, a chaplaincy or bursary in St. Salvator's, and endowed it with the rents of certain houses in South Street, St. Andrews. The holder was to celebrate masses for the souls of the founders and their relations, and of James v., Mary of Guise, and Cardinal Beaton. In 1545 Peter, the Chaplain of St. Salvator, is mentioned as his coadjutor, and Major ceased, from the increasing infirmity of age, to hold any of the annual offices of the University, but retained the Provostship till his death in 1549 or 1550, when he was succeeded by William Cranstoun.

Buchanan spoke of him as already in extreme old age in 1524. This appears to us somewhat of an exaggeration, as he was only fifty-four. Perhaps, as has been suggested, the ordinary limits of human life were counted shorter in that age than in ours. The date of his birth, now precisely ascertained, proves that before his death he exceeded by ten years the term of life allotted by the Psalmist.

James Laing's story of Major and Buchanan. Another reason may be suggested for the censorious tone of all Buchanan's notices of Major. If we could implicitly credit the gossiping and malicious Doctor of the Sorbonne, James Laing, Major had actually taken part in the condemnation of Buchanan for heresy in 1539, because he recommended James v., as it was absurdly put, to eat the Paschal Lamb in Lent, or, as the fact may have been, to break the fast which the Roman Church enforced during that season. 'The king', says Laing, 'summoned the Doctors of Theology at St. Andrews, amongst whom was John Major, a man of the greatest piety and learning in Philosophy as well as Theology . . . and when the question was proposed to him he answered: "He who says, Most Christian king, that you ought to eat the Paschal Lamb wishes you to become a Jew, and to live according to the customs of the Jews, who deny that Christ has yet come or was born of the Virgin. For the Paschal Lamb is an institution of the ceremonial law, and every ceremonial law is dead once Christ has suffered, as the apostle clearly says in the fifth chapter of the Galatians."'[1]

Though this story bears the marks of being largely apocryphal, Cardinal Beaton appears certainly to have been the instigator of Buchanan's imprisonment, from which he escaped, as he tells us in his own Life, while the guards were asleep [2]. When he was again arrested in Portugal, one of the charges against him was that he had eaten flesh in Lent[3], and there is nothing improbable in this having formed part of the earlier accusation in Scotland, or that Major may have been consulted by James v. on the point. If so, Buchanan's dislike of Major had another ground besides his contempt for the logical and sophistical teaching of the Professor.

That the closing years of Major's life were those of enfeebled age is shown by the appointment of a coadjutor, and by the fact that he was excused from attending the Provincial Council of Edinburgh in July 1549, in whose records he is described as Dean of the Faculty of Theology of St. Andrews, on the ground that he was 'annosus, grandaevus, debilis'.[4] Although Buchanan exaggerated, Major's productive life ended with his second residence in Paris. No later work proceeded from his ready pen, and we have scanty notices of what he did in St. Andrews as head of St. Salvator. Perhaps the absence of a press in Scotland capable of producing such works as his, and the occupations of the principal of a College, precluded him from further literary labours. But there were other and deeper causes. The state of Scotland was not favourable to the calm

---

[1] Jacobus Langaeus *De Vita, Moribus atque Gestis Haereticorum nostri temporis.* Paris, 1581.   [2] *G. Buchanani Vita Sua.*   [3] *Ibid.*
[4] Joseph Robertson : *Ecclesiae Scoticanae Concilia,* p. 82.

production or revision of philosophical or theological commentaries. The time for contemplation had passed, the time for action had come. Major was not a man of action. To one who had finally chosen to abide by the old church and yet had fostered some liberal ideas, which he hoped the Church would itself realise, the progress of the Reformation and the means adopted to stifle it must have produced thoughts best buried in silence. It was too late to change his opinions. However liberal in other matters, the Holy Roman Church was still to the venerable Doctor of the Sorbonne the exponent of sound faith in religion. It is seldom that a man of serious thought alters his views after middle age. Had he been twenty years younger it might have been different.

Knox and Major. Two glimpses of Major in his old age are given in the History of the Reformation by John Knox, which show that although he adhered to the old church he was willing to hear its abuses condemned in the strongest language. In 1534 a Friar William Airth preached at Dundee against the abuses of cursing and of miracles, and the licentious lives of the bishops. John Hepburn, Bishop of Brechin, having called him a heretic for uttering such opinions, 'the Friar, impatient of the injury received, passed to St. Andrews and did communicate the heads of his sermon with Master John Mair, whose word then was holden as an oracle in matters of religion, and being assured of him that such doctrine might well be defended, and that he would defend it, for it contained no heresy, there was a day appointed for the said Friar to make repetition of the sermon'. Airth accordingly re-delivered it in the parish church, and amongst his hearers were Major and the other heads of the University. The sermon was on the text, 'Truth is the strongest of all things'. Knox gives its substance, which was certainly bold enough, but as it touched chiefly morals and not doctrine it might escape the charge of heresy. 'One matter', says Knox, 'was judged harder, for he alleged the common law, "That the Civil Magistrate might correct Churchmen and deprive them of their benefices for open vices".'

It shows the critical moment the Reformation had reached in Britain that the same Friar, according to Knox, having escaped to England, was cast into prison by Henry VIII. for defence of the Pope. But Henry, as Buchanan tells us, was then intent on his own ends rather than purity of religion, 'burning men of opposite opinions at the same stake'.

Major at Knox's first Public Sermons.

Major was again present at a still more memorable occasion thirteen years later, in 1547, when Knox first preached in public at the earnest request of John Rough, Minister of St. Andrews, Sir David Lindsay, the poet, and Balnaves, a lawyer, one of the first Judges of the Court of Session. His text was from the seventh chapter of Daniel, 'And another King shall rise after them, and he shall be unlike unto the first, and he shall subdue three kings, and shall speak great words against the Most High, and shall consume the saints of the Most High, and think that he may change times and laws, and they shall be given into his hands until a time and times and dividing of times'.

After explaining the prophecy of the fall of the four empires—the Babylonian, Persian, Grecian, and Roman, he declared that on its destruction rose up that last beast, which he declared to be the Roman Church; but before he began to open its corruptions he defined the true kirk as that which heard the voice of its own Pastor Christ, and would not listen to strangers. Then, grappling more closely than any preacher had yet done with the corruptions of Rome, 'he deciphered the lives of the Popes and of all shavelings for the most part, and proved their doctrine and laws to be contrary to those of God the Father and of Christ'. The reigning Pontiff, we should remember, was Alexander VI., 'that monster', to quote the just condemnation of Villari, whose enormities made even the vices of Sixtus IV. to be forgotten. Knox's crucial instance of false doctrine was the same as Luther's—'Justification by works, pilgrimages, pardons, and other sic baggage, instead of by faith through the blood of Christ which purgeth from all sin.' Treating of the ecclesiastical law he condemned the observance of days and abstinence from meats and marriage, both of which Christ made free. He reached his climax by quoting the claims alleged on behalf of the Pope, as 'That he cannot err, can make wrong of right and right of wrong, and can of nothing make somewhat'. Finally, he said, turning from the congregation to the seats of honour, 'If any here (and there were present Master John Mair, the Provost of the University, the Sub-prior, and many Canons with some Priors of both orders), will say that I have alleged Scripture doctrine or history otherwise than it is written, let them come to me with sufficient witness, and I, by conference, shall let them see not only the original where my testimonies are written, but prove that the writers meant as I have spoken.' Even this daring language would apparently have passed unchallenged had not Hamilton, the Archbishop-elect, written to Winram, the Sub-prior, rebuking him for suffering it. A conference was accordingly held, in which Winram disputed with Knox, but left the brunt of the argument to a Friar Arbuckle, for Winram himself already inclined to the reformed doctrines, which he ultimately adopted.

Major and the Scottish Reformation. To understand the position of Major, the representative of a former generation brought face to face with the ideas and events of the new era, when, in Scotland at least, Reform came so quickly as almost to outstrip the Revival of Learning, we must recal briefly the course of Scottish affairs from his return to St. Andrews till his death.

St. Andrews was then, more than at any other time, a political and religious centre; and, though himself inactive, Major came constantly in contact with the chief actors in the tragedies of which Scotland, not yet finally committed to the Roman or the Reformed Church, became the scene.

The young king, James v., whose tutor and playfellow had been David Lyndsay of the Mount, whose father had chosen Erasmus as preceptor for his bastard half-brother, the Archbishop of St. Andrews, whose confessor, Seton, had imbibed some Reformed doctrines, whose uncle, Henry VIII., had plied him with flattery and promises, wavered, like Francis I., between Rome and the Reformation. He gave signs that he might accept the latter. He set on foot a reform of the Cistercians, the richest and most corrupt of the older orders of Monks. He employed Buchanan to describe the hypocrisy which made even more odious the Franciscans, whose poverty and asceticism had sometimes become the cloak of a still more dangerous licence, threatening the family, and not merely the cloister, with corruption. He had at last succeeded in obtaining a portion of the exorbitant revenues of the Bishops for the foundation of a College of Justice, one of the most urgently needed reforms; for the Baronial and Ecclesiastical Courts rivalled each other in the delay, the cost, and often the denial of justice.

But other influences operating on the unstable mind of James prevailed. In 1534 Henry VIII.'s divorce received the sanction of Parliament. Whoever, knowing the facts, judged it by any but a purely English standard must have begun to doubt whether good morals and justice were always on the side of the Reformers. One of its consequences was to put an end to the project of James's marriage to Mary Tudor, now disinherited. In 1535 he refused to meet his uncle on the English side of the Border, and in March of the following year a treaty of marriage was made between him and Mary de Bourbon, daughter of the Duke of Vendome. In winter he went to France, and, displeased with his proposed bride, pre-

marginal note: James v.

ferred the delicate beauty of Madeleine, the daughter of Francis I.
The Scotch King was received by the French Court with the
honours usually paid only to the Dauphin, and the citizens
of Paris thronged to see him, and receive his largesse as he
passed through the streets of their beautiful capital. Madeleine
having died in midsummer 1537, an embassy, with David
Beaton, Bishop of Mirepoix, at its head, soon negotiated
another French alliance. The choice fell on Mary, daughter
of the Duke of Guise, widow of the Duke of Longueville. This
marriage, celebrated at St. Andrews in June 1538, finally decided the King in favour of the Roman Church. The family
of Guise was devoted to it. The uncle and brother of the
new Queen were Cardinals, and David Beaton secured the
same coveted dignity by promoting the match as Wolsey had
done by a similar service. Roman ecclesiastics of the worldly
type have always been promoters of politic marriages in the
interests of the Church. In 1539, soon after christening the
young prince, the first short-lived fruit of the marriage, in his
cathedral, James Beaton died. He had not been a favourite
with the King, who had even written to the Pope, complaining
of the aggrandizement of this obscure family, but he succeeded
in transferring or leaving his wide benefices to his kinsmen.
His nephew, David, already Abbot of Arbroath, became Archbishop; Dury, a cousin, Abbot of Dunfermline; and Hamilton,
another of his kin, Abbot of Kilwinning. David Beaton now
acquired complete ascendancy in the councils of the King.
He persuaded the clergy to the politic step of making James a
larger grant out of their revenues. As Archbishop he con-
vened an assembly of nobles, prelates, and doctors of theology,
of whom Major was one, at St. Andrews, and pronounced an
oration against the danger to the Church from heretics who
professed their opinions openly even in the Court, where they
had found (he said) too great countenance. Sir George Borth-
wick, captain of Linlithgow, was condemned in absence for

Marginal note: Cardinal Beaton.

denying the authority of the Pope and accepting the heresies of England, and his image was burnt in the Market Place of St. Andrews[1]. Henry VIII. made a last attempt to have a personal interview with his nephew, but Beaton's influence prevented it. A war ensued, in which the defeat of the Scotch under Oliver Sinclair at Solway Moss proved fatal to James, who sank under the blow, and died at Falkland on 14th December 1542, seven days after the birth of Mary Stuart. In spite of a will produced, it was alleged forged by Beaton, appointing him Regent, the Estates chose Arran as next heir to the Crown. Beaton was for a short time put in ward, but made terms with Arran, and became Chancellor in 1543. The failure of Henry's negotiations for the marriage of the infant Queen to his son Edward was followed by Hertford's ruthless raid, which revived the old hatred of the English throughout Scotland. On 1st March 1546 George Wishart was burnt before the gate of the Archbishop's castle at St. Andrews. Four other victims of humble birth had shortly before been executed at Perth. In less than three months, on 28th May, the Cardinal was murdered in his own castle by Norman Lesley and a small band of young men of good family from Fife, some of whom had private wrongs to revenge, but chiefly in retaliation for Wishart's death. Shutting themselves up in the castle, where they received supplies from England, and were joined by persons of like mind, amongst whom was John Knox, they were closely besieged by the Regent's forces, and compelled to agree to terms by which, on receipt of absolution from Rome, they were to surrender the castle. In the meantime the siege was raised, and the son of Arran given them as a hostage. It was during this critical interval that Knox preached the daring sermon at which Major was present. In the summer of 1547 the absolution arrived, but its terms were equivocal, and the besieged refused to accept it. In June, Strozzi, the French Admiral,

Murder of the Cardinal.

---

[1] May 1540.

arriving with a fleet, the siege was renewed. 'Cannons were planted, some on the steeple of the Parish Church, some on the tower of St. Salvator's, and some in the street that leads to the castle.' On 29th July a breach in the south wall forced a capitulation. The besieged saved their lives, but were sent to France as prisoners in the French galleys. The death of Henry VIII. had prevented the coming of an English fleet for their relief. Another raid by Hertford, now the Protector Somerset, followed, and the loss by the Scots of the battle of Pinkie led to the infant Queen being sent to France for safety. Supported by French troops the Scotch were able to make head against the English, and recover the castles which had been lost, and Scotland was made a party to the French peace with England in April 1550. It was probably shortly before its conclusion that Major died.

Death of Major 1550.

Who can wonder that amid such scenes an old man who had survived his generation held his peace. The flames kindled by the Inquisition were being revenged by the dagger of the assassin. Almost the last news he heard was that the Lamp of the Lothians, the fine Church of Haddington, at whose altars he had worshipped, had been burnt; almost the last sight he saw was the flash of cannons on the Castle from the tower of St. Salvator. On the one side stood the Church in which he had been born and bred, the Queen Dowager, his patrons the bishops, and most of his older friends both in France and Scotland; on the other, his ablest pupils and an increasing number of the Scottish people, both gentry and burghers. For the one cause fought the French Monarch and Court, whose brilliant corruption he must well have known; for the other, the English king was defying the laws of his own realm to carry out his will, while his generals were harrying, burning, bombarding the Scottish towns in a manner which recalled the havoc of the wars of Edward I.

The Council of Trent just assembled evinced a desire to

reform the Church from within, and several Scottish bishops, notably Hamilton, the Prelate who succeeded Beaton, were ready to minimise the Roman doctrine and to remedy the most flagrant abuses. To one who could brook a question upon the matter,—who did not see, as the Reformers did, in the Pope Antichrist, in Rome Babylon, in its doctrine idolatry, in its casuistry a root of moral corruption,—still more to one whose inveterate habit it was to argue everything from both sides, there might well seem room for hesitation, for delay, for choosing the older as the safer path. Behind the external tumult, to one who was a theologian and philosopher, living in the world of thought more than of action, there were arrayed on the side of Rome, once its premises were accepted, the forces of Logic and Casuistry, for which he had the affection the adept feels for the weapons of his own craft.

There was also the terror of the stake; for, after all, most men are human. Martyrs are amongst the smallest of minorities in the human race. During the preceding centuries persecution had all but extinguished the doctrines of Wycliffe and of Huss. Even after the revival of learning had borne its natural fruit in the decay of superstition, it arrested the Reformation in Italy and Spain and the greater part of France. Character of Major.

The life whose course from such materials as exist we have followed was not that of a hero or a martyr. But if the character and conduct of Major have been rightly interpreted they have value of their own not to be overlooked. They bring vividly before us the Scottish man of learning as he was in this perilous age, when new ideas and a new faith were clashing with the old not merely in the field of argument but by fire and sword.

Major the lifelong student, and devoted professor, who preferred, as he himself says, 'to teach rather than to preach'; fond of his books; fond of music as the relaxation, and of argument as the business, of his life, but fond also of his pupils Major and Knox compared.

and his country, did what lay within his capacity to improve his pupils and inform his countrymen. But it was beyond his power to reform his age by the potent words, and unflinching courage, which in spite of grave errors make most of his countrymen reverence, and impartial judges of other nations respect, the name of John Knox. The deeper, stronger work of the Reformer has, as it deserved, lasted longer than the work of his master the Schoolman. Even when that part of it which is dogmatic has been superseded, that part of it which is moral will continue, for it rests near the foundations of social and religious life, while that part of it which is national will always remain an integral and crucial chapter in Scottish History. The philosophy and the theology of Major served for his generation only, quickened the thoughts of some of his students by attraction, and of others by repulsion, and then quietly sank into oblivion. Only a stray passage here and there has been brought to light in modern times by the diligent investigator of the progress of European thought or as an aid to the understanding of his character.

Character of Major's History.

'Habent sua fata libelli.' The short history which he probably valued least of all his works has had a longer life. It was reprinted in the last century by Freebairn, and has always been favourably known to students of Scottish History. In the hope that it may reach a still wider circle, the History is now for the first time translated by Mr. Constable, a task rendered difficult from its terse and occasionally abrupt style, but accomplished through familiarity with Major's thoughts, acquired by a prolonged and patient study of his writings and character. An estimate of its chief characteristics has already been given in this sketch of the life of the author. It is not a history to read for new information. History is a progressive branch of knowledge. Much more is known now than Major knew of our ancient annals. But his work will always be interesting as the first History of Scotland written in a critical and judicial spirit, and as presenting the view of that history in its past course and future tendency taken by a scholar of the sixteenth century, who, though he halted in the old theology, was so far as history is concerned singularly far-sighted and fair. Such qualities are not even yet so common amongst historians that we can afford to neglect an early example of their exercise. Æ. M.

APPENDIX TO THE LIFE.

I.—NOTICES OF JOHN MAJOR IN FRENCH AND SCOTTISH RECORDS.

Note.—I am indebted to Monsieur Chatelain of the Sorbonne for an exact copy of the references to Major in the 'Liber Receptoris Nationis Alamanie,' which has been preserved for the years 1494 to 1501. Mr. J. Maitland Anderson, the Librarian of the University of St. Andrews, has done a similar service by making a careful excerpt of all entries relating to Major in the Records of that University. The references to the offices he held in the University of Glasgow have been taken from the printed volume of its Munimenta.

Æ. M.

(1.) *University of Paris.*

Archives de l'Université de Paris. Registre 85.
' Liber Receptoris Nationis Alamanie.'

(Anno 1494).—Sequuntur nomina licentiatorum huius anni.

Johannes Maior dyoc. sanct. Andree, bursa valet 4 sol. 1 lib.

(Anno 1495).—Inter nomina incipientium huius anni :

Dns Johannes Mair dioc. sce Andree cujus bursa valet 4^{or} sol. i. lib. pro jocundo adventu et cappa rectoris. . . . ii. lib.

(At the end of the year 1498, following upon the accounts of the Receiver, *i.e.* 'Robertus Valterson, dioc. S. Andree,' may be seen the signature of the *procureur*, who thus vouched for the Receiver's statement of accounts :—)

Ita est,
Johannes H. Maior.

Anno dominice incarnationis 1501 coadunata fuit Germanorum natio apud edem divi Mathurini ad decem klas octobres super novi *receptoris* electione, ubi pacatissime ut putatur, deo inspirante, delectus fuit magister *Johannes Mair gleguocensis diocesis sanct. Andre.* Qui et receptas et impensas ea serie qua sequitur ut cumque executus est.

The Receiver who succeeded Major, ' Mag. Christianus Hermanni,' was elected in 1502 'in vigilia Sanct. Mathei.'

A° 1506. Lic. (in theol.) Johannes Major, Scotus, de collegio Montano. Ordo Lic. 55 (Bibl. Nat. MS. No. 15440).

[v. Budinsky : Die Universität Paris, 1876, p. 91.]

APPENDIX 89

(2.) *University of Glasgow.*

COPY of a letter of Exemption from Taxation granted by James v. to the University of Glasgow, confirming prior exemption. 20 May 1522.

This letter is said to have been obtained at their own expense 'per venerabilem virum Magistrum Jacobum Steward prepositum ecclesie collegiate de Dunbertane ac Rectorem Johannem Majorem theologie professorem thesaurarium capelle regie Striuilingensis vicariumque de Dunlop ac principalem regentem Pedagogij Glasguensis.' *Munimenta Alme Universitatis Glasguensis, I. p. 47.*

GENERAL Congregation of the University, 3d November 1518.

Amongst others incorporated by the Rector, Adam Colquhoun, Canon of Glasgow, was 'Egregius vir Magister Johannes Major, doctor Parisiensis ac principalis regens collegii et pedagogii dicte universitatis canonicusque capelle regie ac vicarius de Dunlop.' *Ibid. II. p. 133.*

GENERAL Congregation of the University of Glasgow on 24th May 1522, under the presidency of James Stewart, Provost of the Collegiate Church of Dumbarton, and Rector of the University, and John Major being present, who is described as Professor of Theology, Treasurer of the Chapel Royal of Stirling, Vicar of Dunlop and Principal Regent.

The Rector explained the privileges of the University with reference to exemption from taxation. On the same day Major was appointed one of the auditors of the Accounts of the Foundation of David de Caidyow for a chaplaincy at the altar of the Virgin in the Cathedral. *Ibid. II. pp. 134, 144.*

Ibid. p. 143.

AT a General Congregation of the University at the Feast of Saints Crispin and Crispinian, 1522, for the election of a new Rector.

John Major was one of the three 'intrantes' who continued James Steward in the office. *Ibid. II. 147.*

PRESENTATION by James v. of Treasurership of Chapel Royal, dated 1st June 1520, in favour of Mr. Andrew Durie in view of the resignation of John Mair, Professor of Theology and last Treasurer. *Register of the Privy Seal, lib. v. fol. 144. See History of the Chapel Royal—Grampian Club, p. liv. 57-98.*

(3.) *University of St. Andrews.*

[*Maioris—Mayr—Maior—Major* used interchangeably. Usually declined according to the context, *Maioris, Maiorem, Maiore.*]

[ACTA RECTORUM.]

1523, June 9.	Incorporated. [Entry as in Irving's Buchanan.]
1523, Jan. 17.	Elected one of the deputies to visit St. Salvator's College. [Entry as in Irving's Buchanan.]
1524, Nov. 7.	One of the Auditors of the Accounts of the Quaestor of the Faculty of Arts for the year 1523-24.
1524, Feb. last.	Elected one of the Rector's Assessors and Deputies.
1525, Jan. 22.	Elected one of the Deputies to visit St. Salvator's College.
1532, Feb. last.	Elected one of the Rector's Assessors and Deputies.
1533, Jan. 15.	Elected one of the Deputies to visit St. Salvator's College.
1534, Feb. penult.	Elected one of the Rector's Assessors and Deputies.

He was further elected to the same posts on the last day of February 1536; April 30, 1539; March 2, 1539; March 1, 1540.

Elected one of the Rector's Assessors on the last day of February 1541, 1542; one of the Rector's Assessors and Deputies on the last day of February 1543; and (?) 1544.

1545. There was elected as one of the Assessors, 'Petrum Capellanj Domus Saluatoris Prefectj Coadiutorem.'

The *Assessors* were appointed 'ad assistendum eidem domino rectorj et eidem consiliendum.'

The *Deputies* were appointed 'ad exercendum rectoris officium in eius absencia.'

[ACTA FACULTATIS ARTIUM UNIV. ST. AND.].

1523, Nov. 3.	Elected one of the Dean's Assessors [I.M. *Canonicum* capelle regie Stirlingensis].
Mar. 19.	Elected one of the Dean's Assessors [I.M. *Thesaurarius* capelle regie Stirlingensis].
1524, Nov. 3.	Elected one of the Dean's Assessors [I.M. *Thesaurarius* capelle regie Stirlingensis].
1525, Mar. 4.	Named as one of the Dean's Assessors [I.M. *Thesaurarius* capelle regie Stirlingensis].

APPENDIX 91

Elected one of the Dean's Assessors [I.M. *Thesaurarius* capelle regie Stirlingensis].				Apr. 8.
Elected one of the Dean's Assessors [I.M. *Thesaurarius* capelle regie Stirlingensis].				Nov. 3.
Elected one of the Dean's Assessors [I.M. only].				1531, Nov. 3.
Elected one of the Dean's Assessors [I.M. vicarius dunloppij successor prefecti collegij Sancti Saluatoris].				1533, Nov. 4.
Elected one of the Dean's Assessors [I.M. prefecti Coll. Sti. Salu.].				1534, Nov. 3.
Elected	do.	do.	do.	1535, Nov. 3.
Elected	do.	do.	do.	1537, Nov. 3.
Named as	do.	do.	do.	Nov. 10,
Elected	do.	do.	do.	1538, Feb. 1.

REGISTER OF DOCUMENTS CONNECTED WITH ST. SALVATOR'S COLLEGE.

'Maister Jhon Mayr' is first mentioned as 'Prowest of the College,' 1536, May 3. on February 1536, and other references to him as 'Prepositus Coll. Eccles. S. Salvatoris' occur on the following dates: 1540, Feb. 25; 1539, Jan. 9; 1542, May 31; 1544, Aug. 3, Apr. 29, Apr. 30, May 1, May 2; 1543, Apr. 13, Apr. 18; 1535, Feb. 15. None of these entries throw any light on Major's personal history, with the exception of that under Jan. 9, 1539. This is a charter granted by Major in conjunction with William Manderston, founding a chaplaincy or bursary (Capellania seu Bursa) in S. Sal. College (with power to the Rector and his Assessors to transfer it to St. Mary's College)—the holder to celebrate Masses for the souls of the founders and their relations, James v. and Mary his Queen, Cardinal Beaton, etc. The endowment consisted mainly of annual rents of tenements in South Street, St. Andrews.

EXTRACTS FROM THE ACTA RECTORUM UNIV. ST. ANDREÆ.

CURIA tenta per venerabilem et egregium virum magistrum alex- 1540, June 15. andrum balfowr rectorem de Longcardy vicarium de Kilmany almeque vniuersitatis sancti Andree rectorem In capella beate Marie uirginis infra claustrum collegij sancti saluatoris situata martis decimoquinto Iunij In anno domini Jaj vᶜ. xlmo.

In causa exactionum recusatoriorum fore declinatoriarum implice duplice et triplice venerabilis et egregij virj magistri nostri magistri Johannis maioris prepositj collegij sancti saluatoris et domini Johannis

vynchestre capellanj pronund,¹ ante pronunciacionem comparuit prefatus
venerabilis vir magister Johannes mair et contentus fuit quod prefatus rector cognosceret in principali causa domini Johannis vynchestre
contra eum non obstantibus exactionibus prefatis productis per suum
procuratorem a quibus insiluit et admisit prefatum rectorem in Judicem
in dicta causa prout tenore presentis acti admittit et eapropter de con-
sensu partium prefatus rector decrevit pro cedend. in principali causa
veneris super sedendo modificacionem appensa fact. per prefatum dominum Johannem vynchestre qua prefatum prepositum usque ad discus-
sionem principalis cause.

DIE xxvj februarij Anno Domini millesimo quingentesimo
quadragesimo.

1540, Feb. 26. Christi nomine invocato nos Alexander balfour vicarius de Kilmany ac rector alme vniuersitatis sanctiandree Judex in causa et
partibus subscriptis pro tribunali sedentes in quadam causa petitionis
summarie sane cedule querile coram nobis motâ et adhuc pendente
indecisa inter discretum virum dominum Johannem vinschester capellanum actorem ab vna et venerabilem et egregium virum magistrum
nostrum magistrum Johannem maiorem sacre theologie professorem
prefectumque ecclesie collegiate sancti saluatoris intra ciuitatem sanctiandree reum partibus ab altera judicialiter cognoscentes auditus prius
partium predictarum petitione reuersione ceterisque Juribus hinc inde
productis et repetitis per nos visis auditis et intellectis remotis et ad
plenum discussis juxta ea que vidimus audiuimus et cognouimus Jurisperitorum comunicato consilio et sequueltio quibus fidem fieri fecimus
relacionem in eadem solum deum pre oculis habentes eiusque nomine
sanctissimo priusque inuocato per hanc nostram sententiam diffinitiuam
quam ferimus in his scriptis pronunciamus decernimus et declaramus
prefatum venerabilem virum magistrum nostrum magistrum Johannem
mair prepositum ecclesie collegiate antedicte a petetis et in petitione
dictj domini Johannis vinschester capellanj absoluend. fore et absoluj
debere prout absoluimus per presentes necnon obstan allectis pro parte
dictj domini Johannis coram nobis et minime probatis prout ex deductis
coram nobis legitime probatim et compertim extitit dictumque dominum
Johannem vinschester capellanum in expensis litis factis et fiendis eadem
nostra sententia diffinitiua condemnantes Ipsarum tamen expensarum
taxacione nostro judicio in posterum reseruata lecta et in scriptis re-
dacta fuit hec nostra sententia diffinitiua die sabbato xxvj[to] februarij Anno
dominj millesimo quingentesimo xlmo in presentiis Johannis dowglas
henricj schaw domini Johannis young capellani junioris georgij makke-
sone cum diuersis aliis.

---

¹ Perhaps contraction for 'pronuntianda.'

APPENDIX 93

DIE xij mensis Decembris anno domini etc. xlij° lata erat[1] presens 1542, Dec. 12. sententia per infrascriptum rectorem in insula beate marie infra claustrum sancti saluatoris collegij.

Cristi nomine inuocato nos Thomas barklay huius almj vniuersitatis sanctiandree ac de neffa Rector Judexque cause et partibus infrascriptis pro tribunalj sedentes in quadam causa appellacionis a grauamine discretj virj domini Johannis vinsister capellanj a venerabilj et egregio viro magistro Johanne mair preposito collegij sancti saluatoris intra ciuitatem sanctiandree citati contra et aduersus discretum etiam virum dominum thomam Kyneir capellanum [ac ipsum prepositum] appellatos ad nos et nostrum auditorium rectoratus interiect ... si in eadem deuolut ... alias judicialiter ventilata cognoscentes auditis prius partium predictarum petitione respontione allegacionibus processu judicis a quo et ceterisque juribus hincinde productis per nos visis intellectis et ad plenum discussis juxta ea que vidimus audiuimus et concipimus jurisperitorum comunicato consilio et sequuto quibus fidelem fierj fecimus relacionem in eadem solum Deum pre oculis habentes eiusque nomine sanctissimo primitus inuocato per hanc nostram sententiam diffinitiuam quam ferimus in his scriptis pronuntiamus decernimus et declaramus dictum magistrum Johannem Mair prepositum antedictum judicem a quo suas literas citatorias dicto domino Johannj appellantj ad citandum dictum dominum thomam coram sepefato preposito ad exhibendum et ostendendum quendam assertum collacionem vna cum singulis aliis suis juribus si que de capellania vocata de balcolmy [habuit] intra dictum collegium fundata ad effectum videndj et audiendj huiusmodi collacionem et alia jura cassari annullarj et retractarj et propter raciones dandas male et iniuste denegasse ipsumque Dominum Johannem propterea bonum et juste a prefato preposito ad nostrum auditorium appellasse et prouocasse vlteriore que cause principalj cognitionem nobis reseruantes dictumque magistrum Johannem prepositum antedictum eadem nostra sententia diffinitiua in expensis litis condemnantes ipsarum tamen expensarum taxacione nostro judicio in posterum reseruata.

Major's name, as prepositus collegij Sancti Saluatoris, also occurs in a 1544, Oct. 7. document regarding the power of the Rector, etc., dated 7th October 1544. Also in an Absolutio of 1541. See Lee's *Church History*, i. 82, note.

It also appears in separate charters and writs in the possession of the United College under the following dates:—1532, 1534, 1536, 1538, May 15, 1542, 1553. In this last Martin Balfour is named as *Executor of Mr. John Mair*. Martin Balfour was Rector of Duninoch, Bacchelaurius in sacris litteris et decretis, Officialis S. Andreæ principalis in 1542 (Charter Great Seal Reg. 11 May 1542, No. 2662), and is described as 'Professor sacrarum literarum' in Charter 25 Sept. 1542, *ib.* No. 2788.

---

[1] There are two short contracted words here very faint. The first seems to begin with *p*, and the second with *a*. The conjectural reading of 'presens sententia' is due to Professor Mitchell.

II.

NOTE ON THE SCHOOL OF THE TERMINISTS TO WHICH JOHN MAJOR BELONGED. CHIEFLY FROM Dr. CARL PRANTL, *Geschichte der Logik*, Band IV. Leipzig, 1870.

THE series of Terminist Scotists commenced with Nicholas Tinctor[1], who was followed by Pardus[2] and Bricot[3]. A pupil of Pardus and of Bricot, John Major taught at Paris in the college of Montaigu, was an extremely fertile writer, collected numerous scholars round him and excited them to literary activity. While we must refrain from referring to his Commentaries on Peter Lombard and the physical and ethical writings of Aristotle, we find a number of smaller or greater works by him on Logic in which he frequently treated the same subject in new editions. He edited an edition of the Commentary of John Dorp[4] on Buridan[5], to which it is

---

[1] Prantl, iv. p. 198, 199. Tinctor published a Commentary on the *Summulæ* of Petrus Hispanus, which is expressly designed on the title-page as '*Secundum Subtilissimi doctoris Johannis Scoti viam compilatum*,' and a later work, in which he is described as a follower of Thomas Aquinas, is only according to Prantl (note 117) 'a bookseller's puff or advertisement'.

[2] Hieronymus or Jerome Pardus, a lecturer on Logic of the school called by Prantl 'Terminist Scotists.' His *Medulla dyalectices*, 1505, edited by Major and Jacobus Ortiz, is his only known work.—Prantl, iv. p. 246.

[3] Thomas Bricot, who published alone or in collaboration with George of Brussels several logical tracts between 1492-1505.—Prantl, iv. p. 199.

[4] John Dorp's Commentary was first published at Venice 1499, and twice by Major, Paris 1504, folio, and Lyons 1510, quarto. At the close of the latter edition Dorp is called 'verus nominalium opinionum recitator'.—Prantl, iv. p. 237, note 357.

[5] John Buridan, who died not before 1358, was one of the earliest Nominalists, and following Ockham declares Theological Dogma and Philosophy to be incommensurable. 'Metaphysics differs from Theology in this, that while both treat of God and Divine Things Metaphysics does not consider God and Divine Things except in so far as they can be proved and concluded or induced by demonstrative reasons. Theology, on the other hand, holds certain articles of belief as principles without evidence, and considers further what can be deduced from such articles.'—Prantl, iv. p. 15, note 58.

unnecessary further to refer, as he added to Dorp only some short marginal notes. But in addition he composed several treatises which were collected and printed more or less completely, some of them as Commentaries on Petrus Hispanus, and others Lectures he gave in the Faculty of Arts (Libri quos in artibus emisit). At a later date he collected the Logic of Aristotle and the Summulæ of Petrus Hispanus in an *Introductorium*, and finally he added *Questiones* with reference to the old Logic (*Vetus Ars*).

If we first confine ourselves to the order of the collective edition, we find it commences with a treatise *De complexo significabili*, in which he gives, like his master Pardus in his *Medulla*, an affirmative answer to the question as to the existence of complex terms. Then follow two *Libri Terminorum*, in the first of which, after fixing the logical meaning of the word Term, almost all possible divisions of the Term are discussed by means of doubts and their solutions, and in the second book the same subject is treated in somewhat altered order, after which he places *Abbreviationes Parvorum Logicalium*[1]. Next follow the *Summulæ*, that is, a commentary on Petrus Hispanus, where we find in the introduction a reference to Gerson's utterances on the use of logic, and also a ridiculous play of letters with the word *Summulæ*. The contents of this part are a commentary on the first four tracts of Petrus Hispanus, where at the close of the doctrine of Judgment (following Bricot)[2] there is a special explanation of the term *Contingent*, and of the question current since Buridan wrote as to the variation of the middle term[3]. Besides, the subject of the divisions of the Term is again examined, with reference to the views of Marsilius[4], and at the close of the Categories a Tree of the Predicaments is added. In treating of the Syllogism Major repudiates the Fourth Figure as an unnecessary multiplication more sharply than earlier writers. He adduces, like his teacher Pardus, sophistical examples for each Mood. The Topics and the refutation of Fallacies he treats summarily, because especially in the first there is much unnecessary matter.

---

[1] The *Parva Logicalia* were topics which were not treated specially by Aristotle, but deduced by minor authors from passages in his works.—Prantl, iv. p. 204, note 153.
[2] Prantl, iv. p. 203.   [3] Prantl, iv. p. 34.
[4] Not Marsilius of Padua but of Inghen (d. 1396), a leading Professor of Logic at Heidelberg, whose writings are very voluminous, and in general follow Ockham, Buridan, and other Nominalists though with some variations.—Prantl, iv. pp. 94-102.

A second division of the work begins with the *Exponibilia*[1] in which there is nothing new, for he follows Paulus Venetus[2] and Petrus Mantuanus[3]. Then follow the *Insolubilia*, with reference to which the statement of the principles of others affords the chief interest, for in this part also he follows the explanations of Paulus Venetus. The Commentary added to the second Analytic appears in an improper place and calls for no special remark. We have this portion of the work not from the hand of Major but of his pupil Coronel. The *Parva Logicalia* follow in six tracts, from which we learn that they were reckoned a part of the *Vetus Logica*[4] while the *Consequentia* and *Exponibilia* were deemed to belong to the *Nova Logica*.

The contents of this part consists of a controversial exposition of Petrus Hispanus with frequent use of Peter of Mantua and George of Brussels. Finally there is inserted a concise exposition of the *Obligatoria*[5] and *Argumenta Sophistica*, in which we notice a disposition to contest every proposition sophistically, and in addition a monograph on *the Infinite* in which all possible sophisms which belong to this subject are examined. After what has been said it is not necessary to examine in detail the two last-named writings of Major on Logic, for in the *Introductorium* he merely repeats what he had written before, and the *Quæstiones* are only a commentary of the usual kind on the *Vetus Ars* in the sense of the Terminists.

Among the scholars of Major may be named first *David Cranston* of Glasgow, who taught in Paris, and wrote a treatise on *Insolubilia* and *Obligatoria*. As to the first of these, he proceeds

---

[1] The *Exponibilia* were certain words of frequent occurrence in propositions which required to be expounded to avoid ambiguity and sophisms.

[2] Paulus Venetus (d. 1428) is treated at length by Prantl (iv. pp. 118, 140), who considers his writings as marking the most extreme growth of the Scholastic Logic. He commented on the Physics, Ethics, as well as on the Logic of Aristotle.

[3] Petrus Mantuanus, a Logician of the Terminist School, published *circa* 1483.—Prantl, iv. p. 176.

[4] The Vetus Logica or Ars was not the older logic in point of time but that which treated of the remoter or less immediate parts of logic, while the Nova Logica treated of the Syllogisms and its parts and forms.—Prantl, iv. p. 176, note 9.

[5] The Obligatoria was the division of Logic which dealt with disputation. The disputant was obliged either to maintain (sustinere) or reject (desustinere) or to doubt (dubitare) the proposition advanced. Hence the doctrine of Obligations was divided into ' Positio' ' Depositio ' and ' Dubitatio.'—Prantl, iv. p. 41.

APPENDIX

from a statement of the various opinions of others to his own attempt to treat the *Insolubilia*[1] in accordance with the generally accepted rules of Logic.... With the *Obligatoria* he adopts, in comparison with Major, a somewhat modified division of the *Term*, where, for the first time, we meet with an express application of the different sorts of opposition to the doctrine of Concepts. From the same school came *Antony Coronel of Segovia*, a very fertile writer, who wrote a Commentary on the Categories, an Exposition of the doctrine of Judgments and the properties of Terms, under the title of *Rosarium*, an Explanation of the Posterior Analytics of Aristotle, and a monograph on *Exponibilia* and *Fallaciae*. He also revised and completed a tract of his master, Major, on *Consequentia*. ... A second Spaniard bred in the school of Major was *Caspar Lax*. Of his three works, namely *Termini, Obligationes*, and *Insolubilia*, the first is merely a repetition of what Major had taught on this subject. The high self-esteem which the Terminists of the school of Major had reached is shown in a letter of a friend of Lax, Antony Alcaris, which is printed in the treatise of *Obligationes*. In this the 'clear, perspicuous, useful, sweet, and splendid' dissertations of the Modern are contrasted with the 'languid, arid, jejune, obscure, and little pleasing' works of the Ancient Philosophers.... Another scholar of Major was *Johannes Dullart* from Ghent, who wrote *Quæstiones* on the Categories and a treatise on the *De Interpretatione* of Aristotle, in which he shows extensive reading, and his decided partisanship with the Terminists. ... A fellow-scholar of the last-mentioned writer was the Scotchman, *Robert Caubraith. William Manderston*, also a Scotchman, and several other Spaniards of minor note, are described as belonging to the same school.

The reader who desires to follow the intricacies of the mediæval logic must refer for further details to Prantl's exhaustive and learned work.[2] But for the sake of those who may wish to form a general idea of the distinction between the *Antiqui* or *Reales* and the *Moderni* or *Nominales*, and of the position of the Terminists,

---

[1] The Insolubilia were divided into three modes—(1) Those which could not be solved in any way; (2) those which could not be solved because of some impediment; and (3) those which were difficult to solve. As example of the first was given an invisible sound, of the second a stone hidden in the earth, and of the third an invisible sun.—Prantl, iv. p. 40, note 158.

[2] Prantl, iv. p. 174, points out that at the close of the fifteenth century the Terminists were the majority, though denounced by the orthodox Thomists.

as the school of which Major was a leader was called, we borrow from the same writer the following passages :—

'We first notice a continuation of the earlier tendencies in Logic until the year 1472, when we find the definition of the Party differences followed by a development through the Terminist Scotism, which was opposed by a preponderating conservative Thomism. From about the period 1480-1520 (*i.e.* practically Major's period) a long series of the now reigning school of the Terminists appears.' . . .[1] If we direct our attention to Paris, it is easily to be understood that in the Sorbonne only the elder views were permitted. On the other hand, the University had actively participated in the gradual development of the various new opinions, and had even accepted the views of the Terminists. But in 1473, in consequence of the intrigues of John Boucard, assisted by a former Sorbonnist, Johannes A Lapide, the Moderns had been placed under a bann, and their works in the Library had even been chained, so that they could not be read. The doctors called *Nominales* were those who on principle attached extreme importance to the properties of Terms, including the doctrines of *Insolubilia, Obligationes, Consequentia*, while the Realists applied themselves to things and despised the doctrine of Terms [2]. The dispute was therefore, in the first place, one as to the method of Logic, and only in the second place concerned with the metaphysical question as to Universals, with reference to which the Terminists claimed for themselves the praise of strict orthodoxy. In the year 1481 the Royal Edict against the Nominalists was rescinded, and their books were again allowed to be read.

At the time therefore that Major came to the University the Nominalist doctrine had resumed its popularity all the more because of the persecution which it had suffered, and Major's own masters in Logic, Thomas Bricot[3] and Jerome Pardus[4], both belonged to it. The subtleties and sophistries which the new Nominal logic of the Terminists in the hands of Major and his followers ultimately led to, as exemplified in Prantl's extracts from their works, largely justified the contempt which Buchanan and other disciples of the Renaissance bestowed on it. But none

---

[1] Prantl, iv. p. 186.

[2] It was with reference to this distinction, perhaps, that Erasmus stated his apophthegm which appears to contain the truth of the matter : 'Cognitio verborum prior est, cognitio rerum potior est,' though that apophthegm has a wider application than the merely logical controversy of the Schools.

[3] Prantl, iv. p. 199.   [4] *Ibid.* p. 246.

the less was this stage in logical doctrine an attempt to clear the meaning of words from dubiety in the same line which William of Ockham formerly, and Hobbes and Locke subsequently, followed. It was also, as has been generally recognised by historians of philosophy, both through its merits and demerits, one of the auses which led to the dissolution of the Scholastic Philosophy. That Major belonged to this school in Logic (for though he made an attempt to reconcile the Realists and Nominalists, it was, as we have seen, by assuming the principles of the latter) reacted on his philosophical position, and made him incline to the views of Ockham, the works of two of whose followers he edited. But in Theology he claimed to be and was strictly orthodox, and ends several of his theological treatises with the usual formula, that he submitted all he taught to the Church and the Theological Faculty of Paris.

It is proper to keep in view that he was also a Scotist, and promoted the publication of the *Reportata*, an abridgment of the Parisian Lectures of the Doctor Subtilis. Both the followers of Thomas Aquinas and Duns Scotus claimed to be orthodox, and that their philosophy kept within the limits which the Church allowed to the Schools. Perhaps the Scotists were even more vehement than the Nominalists in the assertion of the soundness of their Theological Doctrine, in order to allay suspicions. But the Roman Church, as if by natural instinct, and the historians of philosophy who have regarded the subject from an external standpoint, concur in regarding Aquinas and not Duns as its true champion among philosophers. Scotism is now almost dead, and the present Pope is doing his best to revive the study of Aquinas. But important as Thomas Aquinas is in the history of philosophy, the attempt to restore his old authority as the Master of Philosophy in the nineteenth century is a hopeless attempt. Scholasticism in any form is now impossible.

The Terminists, as the School to which Major belonged was styled, in some respects occupied an intermediate position between the Scotists and Thomists, the Nominalists and the Realists, but with a decided leaning to the former; and Major is frequently claimed by historians of philosophy, as by Tennemann[1] and

---

[1] Bohn's Translation of Tennemann's History of Philosophy, p. 241. Ueberweg does not mention Major by name, but reckons amongst the Nominalists who followed Ockham in the fourteenth and fifteenth century several of his masters: 'John Buridan, Rector of the University of Paris, of importance because of his

Prantl[1], as a Scotist and Nominalist. It was natural that Major should adopt this school. He claimed Duns Scotus as his countryman, for he had no more doubt of Duns's Scottish than Wadding in the following century had of his Irish origin. His chief masters were Franciscans, who believed in Duns Scotus as a member of their own order. And he came to Paris at a time when the Nominalist development of Scotism was the reigning philosophy in the university.

Similar causes led him to adopt (following Ockham, Gerson, and D'Ailly) the anti-papal position of the Gallican Church.

The Franciscans, speaking generally, for there were exceptions, opposed the absolute claims of the Ultramontane Italian Popes. Their doctrine of Evangelical Poverty cut at the roots, as has been well pointed out by Mr. Owen[2], both of the temporal power of the Pope and the excessive wealth of the prelates and some of the ecclesiastical orders. No one accepted more completely than Major this doctrine. Indeed most, though not all, of his opinions which appear to us bold and anti-papal may be traced to this source. In his writings we constantly come across passages which appear to be copied almost word for word from the works of Ockham or of Gerson. It is because of this that he may be considered, as Ockham has also been, an unconscious precursor of the Reformation in spite of his resting finally in all questions of Faith in rigidly orthodox conclusions.

Nor can we overlook the fact that, like so many other Schoolmen, the method he adopted of arguing all questions on two sides, the Yes and No method as it has been styled,—the doubts which he raised and by no means always solved, and the habit of leaving

---

examination of the Freedom of the Will and his Logical works; Marsilius of Inghen; Peter D'Ailly, who while defending the Church Doctrine yet gave the preference to the Bible above Tradition, and the Council above the Pope; and John Gerson, D'Ailly's scholar and friend, who combined Mysticism with Scholasticism.'—*Geschichte der Philosophie*, ii. p. 215. In an instructive passage, too long to quote, he compares Duns Scotus with Kant, and shows how the critical tendency begun by Duns was carried further by Ockham and the Nominalists, ii. p. 204.

[1] Prantl treats Major throughout (iv. p. 247 *et seq.*) as belonging to the Scotist Terminist or Terminist Scotist School.

[2] Dr. Karl Werner, who writes from the Roman point of view, coincides with Mr. Owen on this point, and remarks that Ockham's opposition to the Papacy turned on the dispute raised by the Franciscan zealots as to the vow of poverty.— *Die nachscotistische Skolastik*, Wien 1883, p. 17.

many points to the judgment of his readers, had, what Mr. Owen has called, with reference to the greater names amongst the Scholastics, a skeptical tendency. It is possible to exaggerate this tendency, but it is impossible to deny its existence. He followed Duns Scotus too in submitting all authority, even the authority of the Church in philosophical matters, and especially in the practical and moral department of conduct, to the test of reason and justice. This it is which has caused the 'Subtle Doctor' to be looked upon with suspicion by the Church, and to be regarded by historians of philosophy as the first great dissolvent of the older orthodox scholasticism. Major and the Terminists were less bold in philosophising than Duns, less bold in action than Ockham, but not the less did their writings and the opinions they introduced tend in the same direction. It was no accident which led Major to direct the republication of the Lectures of Duns at Paris and the logical treatises of the disciples of Ockham.

Prantl, to whom we are indebted for the substance of most of this note, but who must not be held responsible for the view taken in it, remarks in the Preface to his fourth volume, after having made a thorough examination of every known work of the logicians of the later period of scholastic logic, that to describe even useless works is not in itself useless if it saves others from a like labour. But this is a too modest under-estimate of his own valuable labours and of the writings of the Schoolmen.

Their method and philosophy were not a mere marking of time, or a retrogression. It is true they were not great original thinkers like the chief masters of Greek or Modern Philosophy. But they conducted a progressive process—a disputation, to use a word which would have been more familiar to them—between Dogmatic Theology, Ancient Philosophy, and Mediæval Thought, which was necessary to the mental development of Europe. ' Mens agitat molem et inter se corpora miscet.' In this development Major took a minor but a distinct part, as will be acknowledged the more his writings are studied with the attention directed, neither to their form, which is thoroughly scholastic, nor to their explicit conclusions, which are completely dogmatic and orthodox, but to their 'obiter dicta' and ultimate tendency.

It was even, we may venture to say, this tendency, which had more free play when he came to write history, that gave its critical, practical, and independent character to his historical work ; for the thoughts of such a man in the ages of Scholasticism were not disconnected, but pervaded by the same method to whatever subject he turned them. This consideration may also justify the length of the present note in a work primarily concerned only with Major as a historian and not as a philosopher.

Æ. M.

www.ingramcontent.com/pod-product-compliance
Lightning Source LLC
Chambersburg PA
CBHW030408170426
43202CB00010B/1537